AFRAID TO HOPE

Discovering the courage to dream again

RICK RIGSBY, Ph.D.

Nancy & Con —

May you always be filled with Hope... Especially Now!

God Bless

Rick R.

Afraid to Hope
© 2018 by Rick Rigsby

Published by Insight International, Inc.
contact@freshword.com
www.freshword.com
918-493-1718

Unless otherwise noted, Scripture quotations are taken from THE HOLY BIBLE, NEW INTERNATIONAL VERSION®, NIV® Copyright © 1973, 1978, 1984, 2011 by Biblica, Inc.® Used by permission. All rights reserved worldwide.

Scripture quotations marked NKJV are taken from the New King James Version®. Copyright © 1982 by Thomas Nelson. Used by permission. All rights reserved.

Scripture quotation marked KJV is taken from the King James Version of the Bible.

Scripture quotations marked NASB are taken from the NEW AMERICAN STANDARD BIBLE®, Copyright © 1960,1962,1963,1968,1971,1972,1973,1975,1977,1995 by The Lockman Foundation. Used by permission.

ISBN: 978-1-943361-46-5
E-Book ISBN: 978-1-943361-47-2
Library of Congress Control Number: 2017961000

Printed in the United States of America.

DEDICATION

This book is dedicated to my loving and supportive family.

To my incredibly amazing sons, Jeremiah, Andrew, Zachary, and Joshua; to my beautiful and talented daughters-in-law, Jeremiah's wife Grace, and Andrew's wife Lauren; and to our adventurously delightful *"they can do nothing wrong"* grandchildren, Jadon and Isabella . . . each of you make me so proud!

This book is also dedicated to my brothers, my marvelous biological brother, Judge Robert Ray Rigsby and his loving family. And to my wonderful adopted brother, Benjamin Alexander Williams, M.D., and his caring family. Your constant love amazes me.

Most of all, this book is dedicated to:

My Darling Wife Janet
Who encourages me to help others . . .
by writing from the heart.

Your love makes me stand a little taller each day.

CONTENTS

ACKNOWLEDGMENTS

I am deeply indebted to John Mason and his remarkable team at Insight International for believing in me and encouraging this project from the very beginning. John, you're an outstanding author, an exceptional publisher, and even better friend. Your valuable editorial expertise is second to none. I especially wish to thank Michelle Mason for her creative brilliance, and Mike Loomis for his assistance in writing this book in general, and clarifying my thoughts in particular.

I owe a great debt to the following people who made significant contributions to this book. My sincere thanks to:

Dean Renninger, Cover Designer
Michelle Oesterreicher, *Michelle O Photography,* cover picture
Vicki Frye, Typesetter
Marilyn Price, Proofreader

Many thanks to the following for their generosity. Without their support, this project would not have been possible.

Lee and Jamie Dunlap
Jack and Carolyn Little
John and Linda Mason

I offer my deepest gratitude to the following Rick Rigsby Communications staff and our valued partners:

Janet Rigsby, Managing Partner
Lauren Rigsby, Resource Specialist
Fran Metzger, Executive Assistant to the Leadership Team
Mark Pyatt, Business Consultant
Kevin Breeding, Business Strategist and Media Platform Development
Brendan Stocking, *Soxbox, Inc,* Technical Support
And to my Prayer Team!

INTRODUCTION

If you can't fly, then run.
If you can't run, then walk.
If you can't walk, then crawl.
But whatever you do,
You have to keep moving forward.
—Martin Luther King, Jr.

One day, a long time ago, a country woman from Oklahoma met a southern gentleman from Texas. They fell in love, were married, had children, and began a wonderful life together in the San Francisco Bay Area city of Vallejo.

The mother was a formidable power. Her charismatic presence and unshakable determination constantly moved her family forward. The father was a quiet tower of strength. And although he was a third-grade dropout, he would become the wisest man in town, or anywhere for that matter.

Those folks were my parents. What they built was much more than a home for my brother and me. They built a foundation based on love and hope. The Bible was the centerpiece of that hope, as faith and family became supreme values.

But what I never realized as a child, is profoundly clear today. My parents were never afraid to hope. It was hope that raised expectations. It was hope that motivated choices. It was hope that pushed us out of our comfort zones. It was hope that demanded our best. It was hope that sustained our lives.

"Son," my dad often said, "never lose hope." I had no idea of the profound impact of his words and how they would encourage forward momentum in the years to come, especially during a season when the last thing I desired was to move forward.

So, why write a book on hope?

Simple. Look at our world. Stream the news. Google the latest headlines. Download your favorite columnist. Read the paper. I have never seen the need for hope greater during any other time in my life.

A dear friend once mentioned that hopelessness is killing the human race, and it is a very slow and painful death. But, that doesn't have to be the case. Read carefully the words of Helen Keller:

Hope sees the invisible, feels the intangible, and achieves the impossible.

As I have met people in my travels, I am convinced that most of us *want* to hope. The problem is we're afraid. We need to rediscover *how* to get over that fear and hope again.

What if I were to tell you that a few years ago, I experienced the worst season of my entire life . . . only to discover that hope was always there!

Discouraged and disillusioned and mired in self-pity, the circumstances of my life screamed "NO" to the question of whether I would move on. But amidst the shouts, hope was whispering, "Maybe . . . just maybe." As incongruent as this may sound, hope appears most accessible where you least expect it.

That's why I wrote this book.

Allow me to be a tour guide to help you navigate from hopeless to hopeful. Parts of the tour are ugly, raw, and messy. Such is the case with human emotions and unresolved issues. But I guarantee you, if you hang in there and continue reading, you will be rewarded with the realization that maybe . . . you can expect a better outcome for your life.

It's been said that when the world says *give up*, hope says *rise up!*

Dear reader, my *earnest hope* for you is despite the struggle in the valley, or the success on the mountaintop, despite wherever disillusionment, disappointment, or doubt may find you, that this book would place a demand upon you to consider no longer being *Afraid to Hope.*

Dr. Rick Rigsby

Chapter 1

SOMETHING IS MISSING

Circumstances never leave you the same.

Do you agree?

Now let me ask, did the statement make you think of negative events or positive outcomes in your life? I bet I can guess. Two decades ago, I couldn't even imagine a positive reading of those words. After all, stuff happens. And we've all experienced plenty of ... stuff.

Whether it's a problem at work, a family matter or an unexpected tragedy, a sense of resignation and dread can overwhelm us in a moment's notice. Many of us are in survival mode, or at least not living our moments anywhere near to the fullest. Being afraid to hope can paralyze and result in us just going through the motions.

One essential element makes the difference between living and existing. It's astonishing that few of us know anything about it. The purpose of this book is to help you discover the power of hope, and how to make it a dynamic part of your everyday life.

My journey to discovering hope began as a college freshman.

The power of the microphone

The *Id, the Ego and the Super Ego* was the focus of my first class in Psychology 101 at California State University, Chico—a quaint college town nestled at the base of the Sierra Nevada foothills ninety miles north of Sacramento.

I was on my way to fulfilling my *mother's* dream that someday her son would be a psychologist. But everything changed for me one night as I walked through campus with a group of friends. During that walk, we passed an office window and inside we observed a guy, who appeared to be a student, wearing headphones and talking into a mic. We knocked on the window and asked if we could come in. He waved us in, and we realized this was our campus radio station. As soon as I had the chance, I asked a question.

"You get paid to talk?"

"You bet!" was the disc jockey's response.

"This is the job for me," I said.

Following that late night walk through Chico's pristine campus and the encounter with the DJ, I immediately switched majors from psychology to something that back in 1974 was known as *mass communications.*

I have one gift, and that's the ability to talk. And so, I quickly became a volunteer for KCHO Radio, FM 91, Chico State's campus radio station. I loved radio, and within a short time I had my own radio show every Friday night called "Soul Explosion." It could've been called "Rigsby's Talking Explosion," but I was hooked and began to learn the valuable art of ad lib.

A few years later the local CBS television station in Chico, KHSL, offered internships and I was selected and given an opportunity … to try everything! The wonderful thing about a small market station was I could explore every aspect of television production, whether I was ready or not.

Opportunities are limitless at a non-union television station. For example, I was a cameraman on a kids' cartoon show, a driver picking up tapes of syndicated shows, a teleprompter operator, a coffee runner for the anchors—basically anything the station needed. Occasionally, I experienced *intern nirvana:* when an on-air reporter asked me to tag along and maybe run the camera!

I soon realized the people who were advancing were the ones who made themselves available. So, I remember telling my parents, "Sorry, I'm not coming home for Christmas break because I might get a chance to do some studio work as a camera person or run the teleprompter."

For two years I paid my dues, got along with people, listened, and learned. During the last month of my senior year in college the station offered me my dream job: a general assignment television reporter. My first time on the news was the night before my college graduation. Family arrived in town for my graduation, and I'll never forget the look of pride on their faces as their boy delivered the news!

Circumstances were great. My future was bright. The sky was the limit. The year 1978 would become one of my best. First, I land my dream job as a television reporter, then graduate from college, and most important, I marry my college sweetheart—Trina Williams from Lompoc, California—who attended Chico State because of its outstanding nursing program. Trina would become a labor and delivery nurse, as I reported on the daily news. Other than student loans, we were living the "American Dream"!

Fast forward

Life as a television reporter was exciting. No two days are the same, and every day was thrilling as we battled our archenemy: the clock! On Monday morning, you may interview the local police chief about how budget cuts will affect the department, and later that afternoon, you're interviewing an iconic star that's in town as part of a promotional tour. I was often amazed how the most mundane story could take on a life of its own.

For example, in the early 1980s, I was assigned to cover the opening of a new brewery in Chico—if memory serves correctly, the first brewery in the North State. Being the *first* was about the only newsworthy angle we could find. However today, *Sierra Nevada Brewing Company* is among the top breweries in the United States and known worldwide. Covering its genesis and tracking its explosion was thrilling. I do miss my front row seat, watching history unfold.

While journalism has changed, small-market television in the 70s and 80s meant the reporter did everything—from tracking down stories, to scheduling interviews, to "packaging" the story with video sandwiched around interviews. Even the "standup" that features the reporter talking directly to the camera was done solo, by framing the shot, turning the camera on and hopefully standing within the frame. In fact, the very first time I appeared on national television was while doing a standup. A gust of wind blew my camera over and viewers watched a frantic reporter trying to save his camera—and his job. The clip ran all over the world. In America it was featured on the 80s show *Bloopers, Blunders, and Practical Jokes* starring Dick Clark and Ed McMahon!

Listening and telling stories

I met every kind of person from all walks of life. I learned to conduct myself professionally, and retain a high level of composure— whether talking with rice farmers or the San Francisco 49ers following a super bowl victory. I learned how to take large volumes of information and communicate it clearly. I forced myself to go beyond the shallow superficial realm of hearing—what most people do—and actually memorize what people said.

I had no idea at the time, but I was developing a photographic memory. While some may be born with one, I actually developed my mind through the repetitive exercise of remembering names, faces, and facts.

But the most useful skill that helped me be successful was something I learned from my parents: to realize that all people are worthy of dignity and to never be afraid to interact. This practice produced amazing friendships based on trust, which afforded me a variety of "reliable sources," from barbers, to jailers, to airline executives, to a local handyman.

I became a professional storyteller. It's something I've done in every job since—my time at the campus radio station, to a college professor sharing with students the role of the black church in American history, to telling stories to football players at Texas A&M about lessons I learned from a third-grade dropout, to narrating biblical stories as a minister to congregations, to telling stories to audiences worldwide as a motivational speaker about how to live a greater life! It all began with a simple walk through campus one night. In the four decades since, I have learned a fundamental fact about life: Human beings not only love, but learn from stories—whether in speeches, movies, or books. And the better you can tell that story, the greater the potential to connect and impact an audience.

If there was a downside to my television career, it may have encouraged the growth of an already healthy ego! Television news—at least during my era—focused less on context and substance, and more toward the shallow and sensational. Here's my point: to me TV reinforced *image over impact*, and I became a master at creating image. Little did I realize at the time the devastating effects this shift would have on my personal life.

Life became all about impressions. It was all about building or constructing reality—sometimes an alternate reality. My goal became presenting my best self, even if my "best self" was not my current reality. Appeasing the sensibilities of others today sort of reminds me of the minstrel singers of old, who simply *performed* for the masses. The problem was, I wasn't just performing on television, but on the stage of life as well.

Years later, when my circumstances changed, I used this impressionistic way of life to create my version of reality, rather than deal with what was actually taking place. This was no fault of the television industry; it was a fault of mine.

Transitions

With over 30 years to reflect on my television career, I clearly see that despite the few negatives, those were phenomenal years of preparation for what was to come.

Even if you don't know what your purpose is, know this: You're always being prepared for your purpose. Always. People always ask me, "Rick, when will my big break come?" I respond by saying that is the wrong question to ask. The better question is, "Will you be prepared when your opportunity comes?" Right now, examine your experiences— both the good and bad—and you will see a connection as to how circumstances never left you the same. You may even see how they have contributed to who you are and what you do today.

Throughout my career in television—while battling deadlines and working long hours—I never imagined that one day I would communicate all over the world in a variety of different settings. I couldn't have dreamed a video of a graduation speech I delivered would go viral in 2017 with over 130 million views.

And I never imagined I'd write this book. Especially a book on hope.

Before long, my perspective on news and my desire to make it a priority began to change. Trina and I were married four years before our first child was born. Jeremiah Benjamin Rigsby, my "Little Buddy," instantly changed our values. Trina retired from nursing to be a full-time mommy. And that exciting television gig—was becoming less thrilling as holidays, birthdays, and special occasions often were placed on hold. Having to say good-bye to Mommy and Little Buddy to go to work on Christmas morning had lost its magic.

I recall on one occasion that before going on a long-awaited camping trip in the foothills, a news director instructed me to take a news scanner in the event that a breaking story occurred near our camp-site. In addition to the lack of margin, watching a home burn to the ground, and shoving a microphone into the faces of survivors to ask how they felt no longer appealed to me. And while I loved so many of my stories, especially feature reporting or opportunities to cover the San Francisco Giants or Oakland A's, I was no longer willing to pay the price of lost family time.

My dream job was conflicting with my family relationships. The energy, immediacy, and power of visual communication were still there but my view of them had changed.

When I received an unexpected job offer, it had my full attention.

Some former professors casually asked: "How would you like to teach communication courses as a full-time lecturer at your Alma Mater, California State University, Chico?"

The move would double my salary; I'd be home in the summer and on the weekends. I would be home on Mother's Day, July 4th, Thanksgiving, and Christmas. A six-week winter break between semesters? You gotta be kidding!

The offer sounded too good to be true. Apparently, my exposure in the local media was a real plus to the school in general, and its communication department in particular. But there was a problem. I barely made it through college as an undergraduate. Let's be real: I wasn't the brightest guy in the room, and that hadn't changed much in my years away from school. Despite my academic fears, I jumped at the opportunity and gave it a try. After all, the job still centered around talking and telling stories.

But I never anticipated what would happen in this new job. I absolutely loved teaching those young minds about the practical aspects of communication. That was surprise number one.

The second surprise was about me as a graduate student. Part of the job package was the opportunity to work on my Master's Degree. At age thirty-one, I discovered how much I loved learning. I quickly realized that my experience as a reporter awakened my curiosity and expanded my capacity for knowledge. God never wastes a step in our preparation.

Two years later, I gave the commencement address as a graduating Master's student, packed up the family, including our second son Andrew David Rigsby, and headed to the University of Oregon with a scholarship for a Ph.D.

Rhetorically speaking

Rhetoric is the antiquated term for the process of communicating. My studies at Oregon focused on rhetorical theory, the rhetoric of protest movements and of course critical media studies. A few years later with degree in hand, Trina and I once again packed up the car with our children, and a few more books, and headed to my first post-doctorate job as an assistant professor in the Department of Speech Communication at California State University, Fresno.

All-night study sessions and little time for family were now in the rearview mirror. As the movers packed our belongings, we said good-bye to friends in Eugene who had become dear to us. Our tears turned to smiles that August day as we drove south on Interstate 5 and into our new lives. The year was 1990, and the Rigsbys were on top of the world!

With every new adventure, I simply knew good things were ahead—whether it be marriage, career, or the birth of our sons. In every opportunity and new experience, I expected my life to be changed for the better.

Circumstances were treating me pretty well. I had no reason to be afraid. I was in control, on the mountaintop, and looking for other mountains to climb.

Momentum

The Speech Communication faculty at Fresno State became instant family and welcomed us with open arms. We thoroughly enjoyed Fresno and all the civic and campus activities—including watching Bulldog football games featuring Trent Dilfer, my former student and future NFL Super Bowl winning quarterback.

Weekends were spent with church activities, soccer games, and exploring the three national parks just a few hours from Fresno: King's Canyon, Sequoia, and Yosemite. And, most important we now were just a few hours from Trina's family in Lompoc and my folks in the San Francisco Bay Area. The fall of 1990 was a fairytale. Little did we know that in just a few months our fairytale would turn into a nightmare.

After enjoying an amazing Christmas with family, Trina joined me on a faculty retreat on California's beautiful Monterey coast. It was January 1991. The only thing I remember from that trip was how joyful

Trina was. She exclaimed gleefully to me that she was happy, content, and so excited about our future.

Two weeks later, she discovered a lump in her breast during a self-examination. The discovery was diagnosed as breast cancer. I can remember being in the doctor's office with Trina. We heard the words, but could not process them. How could a perfectly healthy 35-year old mother of two be sick? I fully expected any minute to wake from this horrific dream.

Shattered. Devastated. Speechless. We literally were in shock as we drove home. Then, it hit us with the weight of an elephant: We have to tell our children—Jeremiah, age nine, and Andrew, age six. It was the worst Friday afternoon in the world.

The details of those few hours shall remain forever among the four of us. A profound sense of sadness and despair had suddenly replaced a home of joy and laughter. Protecting our boys from the grim reality of an aggressive cancer that threatened the life of their mommy became an impossible task. The boys would have to grow up faster than most, and deal with stuff no child should have to face. We had to be honest with them, yet hopeful that God could heal Mom. Actually, trusting God that He would heal Mom was the only way we kept our sanity.

And, I was mad at God. I was His *golden boy*. How else do you explain a television job before graduation, marrying my college sweetheart, having two amazing sons, the opportunity to attend graduate school, then landing a peach of a job as an assistant professor. *And now God ... You're going to threaten my happiness, comfort, and lifestyle with a sick wife?* That's exactly how I felt. Also, I had a difficult time rationalizing the suffering considering that I was "a good Christian and a minister." Frankly, me and the boys did not deserve this.

It's shameful for me to write, but truthfully, I made Trina's illness all about me. It got worse.

Trina's surgery also revealed that the cancer had invaded the lymph nodes, and required an aggressive treatment plan including not only a mastectomy, but various chemotherapies, radiation, and endless doctor visits and overnight hospital stays. Our lives were no longer our own, and I found myself growing in resentment. Now, scheduling doctor visits and procedures and chemo treatments put an end to family spontaneity. Trips, vacations, even daily routines were put on hold, all subject to treatment schedules. I was angry and fearful as I felt my life spiraling out of control. My new reality was reaffirmed with each new day that offered uncertainty, compounded by frustration and fear. Frankly, until January 1991, I don't ever recall having a bad day. Ever.

Trina was a trooper. We made it through her surgery, and she began chemotherapy once her strength returned. We settled into a schedule that was anything but set. There was no choice. There were good days and dark days, and we learned to be thankful for anything we could, mostly because of a strong support community including my colleagues, Fresno Christian School—the boys' school—and our church, Valley Christian Center.

The drift

Logically, I understand that good things, even innovation can come from crisis. However, in the midst of crisis the thought of anything but pain and disappointment is doubtful. It's hard to have an expectation of innovation, promise, or adventure when you're in the midst of the struggle. Who has time to consider innovation or changing the world when all you're trying to do is survive another dreadful day?

For the first time in my life, Trina's diagnosis was causing me to drift into a deep pit of negativity. I was no longer familiar with the man in the mirror, the words he spoke, or the thoughts he had. Drift.

When Steve Jobs was trying to hire John Scully away from Pepsi™ to run Apple™, Steve asked him, "Do you want to sell sugared water for the rest of your life? Or do you want to come with me and change the world?"

Change the world? Wow, that's a gutsy statement. And they did change the world.

Innovation, in companies and in our personal lives, is an indicator of how we view the future. Those who expect their circumstances to work out for good are those who will continue to grow, overcome, and inspire others.

When I believe the future holds immense promise and adventure, I live differently. I take risks and explore options. I listen to my heart. My world is big.

But look around today. Do you see that kind of expectancy on the rise, or on the decline, in our society? What about in your own life? (Yes, I ask a lot of questions. That's the professor talking.)

In my psychology studies, I learned something about basic human nature, and what we tend to drift toward: 1) the pursuit of pleasure, and 2) the avoidance of pain.

But when I believe the best is behind me, I wall myself off, avoid pain, and pursue fleeting pleasure. My world becomes small, and gets smaller by the day.

I've never seen less positive expectation in society today—even among people of faith. The polls document a decline in optimism. A growing number of people believe our country's best days are behind her, and believe their children will have less opportunity than they had.

How is this possible?

I understand, actually. Our view of life can drift into negativity when circumstances seem to conspire against us and those we love.

It could be a series of disappointments, from experiencing a difficult roommate in college, to being laid off from a job, to walking through the termination of a relationship. Or you might be facing unimaginable heartbreak and tragedy.

When life doesn't go our way, circumstances can cause us to trust only in ourselves. We stop trusting others. *I trust in me because God let me down.* We question why. We start controlling our lives. Or try to anyway.

Stop and think about it. Is there anything more futile than trying to control life? Yet we try, don't we?

But I don't condemn, because I've been there, done that. I bought the XXL t-shirt that says on the front, "I'm in pain." And I wore that shirt proudly for too many years.

I'm fine

Psychologists say the avoidance of that which produces pain is among the most powerful of all human impulses. When I couldn't face unimaginable pain, I tried to self-medicate to avoid it.

In the process, I lost sight of the *one essential element* we all need to live well on this earth.

This book is two decades in the making. What I'll share is deeply personal and frankly, quite embarrassing. But it's for you. If what I've learned can help just one person, it's worth it. You are worth it.

So far, you've read the resume—the highlight reel. But there's so much more beneath the surface. That's true for me and true about you.

So many people I've spoken with over the years seem fine but are really doing their best to survive. You might be concealing a heart filled with pain, or experiencing the drift of disappointment.

Maybe life is good for you right now, but you can't seem to find peace about the past or spark for the future.

Circumstances don't leave us the same way they found us. You're either better or worse, but never the same. Don't pretend otherwise.

This is why the choices we make in those circumstances are so important. And this is why every human being needs to reconnect with one vital element of the human spirit.

By and large, the world is missing it. I was missing it, and maybe you are as well.

It's the difference between resignation and fight. It's the energy to ask, *What if circumstances could leave us better than they found us— every time?*

For the first time in my life, I found myself *afraid to hope.*

Chapter 2

THE VALLEY

Trina and I had finally made it.

Following years of study and struggling to make ends meet during school and away from family, we were back in California. I was employed and our family was thriving. There was just one problem, and it loomed larger than life. Literally.

Trina went through endless rounds of chemotherapy treatments while we rode an emotional roller coaster. Had it not been for our faith in God and the support of family and friends, I doubt we would have made it.

There were tough times that speak to the reality of battling cancer. But there were some good times as well. We took full advantage of those intervening times between treatment cycles when Trina felt fairly decent. Sometimes it was going for a ride to Yosemite, or a picnic in the park. On other occasions, we would see Trina's family in Lompoc or my parents in the Bay Area. Mostly, we lived in the moment. This was not the time to take one second for granted.

However, there was escape from Trina's seemingly inevitable cycle of sickness.

Chemotherapy rounds were followed by radiation treatments, creating a lifestyle revolving around her wildly fluctuating energy levels. Despite the advanced diagnosis, and all the change we experienced in a short time, Trina and I trusted God and simply knew she would be healed. Her brief respites of "feeling better" reinforced our belief. She had good doctors and a fantastic support network. The last thing on either of our minds was moving to Texas.

Texas calling

I'll never forget the call in the spring of 1992 from dear friend, Dr. Marty Medhurst—one of the top national scholars in Rhetoric and Public Affairs, and editor of the journal that bears the same name—and a professor in the Department of Communication at some school called Texas A&M University. He simply called to encourage me to apply for an opening. I shared with him about Trina and our situation and he fully understood. As a man of faith, Marty said, "Just pray about it and we'll go from there."

Not much to pray about. My father is a Texan. My relatives live in Texas. Some of my fondest childhood memories were loading the Rambler station wagon and driving 1,600 miles from San Francisco to Huntsville, Texas! But living there? I had a thousand reasons not to even pray about this. At the top of the list was Trina's health, with the sweltering Texas heat being a close second. And when I mentioned the possible move to sons Jeremiah and Andrew, forget about it. "No way" I believe were their exact words. But, for some strange reason, the thought of a new beginning would not leave my heart. Eventually Trina would arrive at the same conclusion.

After praying about Marty's invitation, Trina and I agreed that just *visiting* Texas for an interview had strategic advantages. Maybe I'd do well enough to get a job offer, and use the offer as leverage with Fresno

State. The icing on the cake for the Texas trip would be a 45-minute drive from College Station to Huntsville and enjoy time with all my relatives including "Mamo" (pronounced *Mam-Maw*), my then ninety-year-old grandmother. I boarded that plane in Fresno with a wife sending me to interview, confident I'd return with an offer and little else. I was not prepared for what happened in the Lone Star State.

After I landed in College Station and recovered from the rodeo ride on a twin-engine turboprop airplane, I fell hard for the campus and the wonderful people in the department. Marty said there was word that former President George Herbert Walker Bush was considering A&M as a possible school for his presidential library—an intoxicating opportunity for faculty in every discipline and for me, an opportunity to closely examine the intersection between the Bush presidency, the media, and civil rights legislation. I fell in love with College Station in general and Texas A&M in particular. After several days of interviews, I flew back to Fresno, and spent the entire flight back working on a new sales pitch to deliver to my family. Trina met me at the airport, and when she asked, "How'd it go?" I responded, "I think we need to talk." In a rare display of disapproval, Trina didn't say another word and walked ten feet ahead of me down the long corridor of the Fresno Airport. Back home, things went from bad to worse, as the boys mounted massive protests over the possibility of leaving their friends, Fresno Christian School, and most of all their California lifestyle.

A&M was gracious and allowed us time to pray and think about a decision. After a few days and to my surprise, Trina said, "For several reasons, I feel this is a move we need to make."

Over the hump

I immediately sprang into action to make a compelling case for the boys to consider. I called every Texas waterpark, amusement park, and kid-friendly attraction and had them send promotional materials to our sons. It worked.

Despite their concerns about having to ride a horse to school, and other over-used geographical stereotypes, the boys were excited. We said a tearful good-bye to friends in Fresno, loaded up the car, and moved to College Station, Texas. I began my career at A&M in the fall of 1992. Although Trina was undergoing chemotherapy, we were excited by a fresh start and felt energized by the hope of a new beginning.

Within a week of being in College Station, we had made best friends for life with medical doctors Haywood and Noreen Robinson, who upon hearing that our home would not be ready for two weeks, insisted that we move in with them and their two girls! Haywood's mother, affectionately known as "Mama" cared for everyone, and was particularly fond of and protective of Trina. We found a church, a Christian school for the boys, doctors for Trina, and a network of supporting friends—all before moving into our new home.

Trina, who had retired to remain home with our sons, had started volunteering at the boys' school in Fresno and continued that tradition at their new school. Despite the ups and downs of chemotherapy treatments, hospital visits, and low energy, she would eventually become the school librarian. The transition to College Station, Texas, could not have been any easier.

Trina loved her role as a librarian at the boys' school—Brazos Christian. We took her favorite wooden rocking chair—the one she sat in when she read at home to Jeremiah and Andrew—to the school where she read to the eager students. Being a librarian gave her such joy and purpose, while taking her mind off treatment schedules and doctor visits.

As we settled into our new life in Texas, the reality that we would stay a few years and then perhaps return back to the west coast began evaporating. We fell in love with Texas. Trina was receiving great care, the boys were thriving, and I experienced an unexpected opportunity.

While on an airplane, I met legendary A&M football coach R. C. Slocum—a providential meeting on several levels. He mentioned his desire to create a coaching position that addressed the development of life skills for his players. Though we agreed to visit later, my heart was intrigued by one thing Coach said: "When I am finished coaching, I will not be judged on wins or losses but on how my players turn out. I want to help them be successful in life."

Coach Slocum and I continued to talk about the position while he allowed me to do chaplain work as a way of providing a spiritual dimension for the team. This also gave me the opportunity to build relationships with the players and earn their trust. After the Departments of Communication and Athletics worked out a joint appointment contract, I officially began working for the football team in 1996. Not having any kind of character or life skills curriculum, Coach Slocum and I agreed that the profound lessons I learned from my father—a wise man who happened to be a third-grade dropout—would be the perfect foundation for our players.

I mention this episode, because that simple visit on an airplane would not only help Coach Slocum accomplish his goals, but our family benefited greatly. That football program became a second family, and provided a great diversion for a family struggling with the realities of a terminal disease.

Sometimes hope appears … where you least expect it.

Deeper into the valley

In September of 1996, I flew from Texas to speak at a church in Rocky Mount, North Carolina, for a Friday night event. Trina was the type of person who never pushed her own agenda, regardless of her situation or how poorly she felt. And this day was no exception. Despite being weak, she forcefully encouraged me not to worry about her and to fulfill my obligation to speak at the church. Following several assurances that she would be fine and would rest under the care of Mama Robinson, I decided to fly to Rocky Mount. On Saturday, I called Trina to check on her. I told her the event went well and I was on my way to the airport. I told her I loved her, and would be home in a few hours. At the time, I had no idea that phone call would be the last time I would ever hear Trina's voice.

I arrived back to College Station late Saturday evening. As I drove down our street, I noticed the normally dark cul de sac was vividly illuminated with the lights of an ambulance and fire truck. I immediately assumed one of our neighbors was experiencing a medical emergency. Then, to my horror, I noticed the vehicles were parked in front of my house.

I dove through the door, passing all the responders, desperately trying to find my wife and children. I was directed into our bedroom to witness a sight that continues to haunt me to this very day.

Trina, my wife of nearly twenty years and the mother of our two young sons, was on the floor as a team of paramedics frantically sought to revive her. I fell to my knees and looked up at the concerned faces, praying to see a glimmer of hope.

Trina had been diligently cared for by Mama Robinson, who loved Trina like a daughter. Mama was quiet, head bowed. Her granddaughters Udelle and Riva, and our sons, Jeremiah and Andrew, wept quietly. We all knew—but we didn't want to know. We didn't want to believe what we were watching.

Attached to breathing equipment, paramedics carefully loaded my sweetheart into the ambulance. Since I wanted to stay near our boys, I was instructed to drive behind the ambulance. The three-mile trip to the hospital felt like three hundred.

The surreal sight of a night sky lit by the beacon of an ambulance transporting my wife was overwhelming. I fought for glimpses of Trina through the rear glass door of the ambulance. My eyes were only able to make out the appearance of a controlled frenzy of activity. Our sons said very little, I just remember saying to myself, O God, please no. Please no. Please don't take her. Not now!

We arrived at the hospital around 11:30 that Saturday night. While attendants worked to recessitate Trina, we were led to a waiting room. After about thirty minutes, which seemed like an all-night vigil, a doctor emerged from the emergency room. His face told me our worst nightmare had become reality.

Shortly after midnight, September 8, 1996, the doctor whispered, "I am sorry." My knees felt weak and my gut felt as though someone had just kicked it. Jeremiah and Andrew had the glazed look of shock and disbelief. Their precious young faces were frozen, and tears streamed from their eyes.

We tried to collect ourselves as best we could. But the fact is, there's nothing to prepare to say good-bye to a mom and to a wife.

We always knew that Mom *could* die. But we prayed day and night that God would heal her, and firmly believed she would live a long life despite the poor diagnosis. When we heard the words, "I am sorry" our sons lost their mommy and I said good-bye to my soulmate.

After a few minutes, medical personnel allowed us to enter the hospital room and say good-bye to Trina. As we gathered around her bed, she looked as though she was asleep. There was peace on her face. It was as if we were in the presence of an angel. We were.

For Trina, the battle was finally over and she was in heaven. For us, the battle was just beginning, and we felt as though we were standing in hell.

I recall our boys saying good-bye to their mom. We stood by the hospital bed for a long while, talking softly and saying our good-byes. Mom was gone. My sweetie had left. We looked at this angel who fought so valiantly. She didn't want to leave us. She did not want to leave her boys motherless. But in an instant, she was gone.

I would learn later that the nearly six years of chemotherapy, radiation, and surgeries required to battle Trina's breast cancer had taken a fatal toll on her precious heart. And just like that, a home once filled with joy and laughter was now furnished with grief, devastation, and emptiness.

Just words

I don't remember walking out of the hospital to the parking lot in the early hours of September 8th. Someone had taken the boys home earlier, but I simply couldn't leave the hospital. Even though Trina had departed this earth, my instincts as a husband caused me to rationalize that she still might need me.

The only thing I remember clearly is sitting in the passenger seat of my car with my close friend and mentor, Reverend Dwight Edwards, who in a few days would preach Trina's funeral.

We sat in there for an eternity after he drove me home. He said very little, and we both cried. I cried uncontrollably. Rational thinking would now elude me for some time. All I wanted was "normal," something rarely found in valleys.

I don't remember most of my conversation with Dwight in those early morning hours. But the one thing I clearly recall was a statement he made.

"Rick, I don't know why Trina died, but I know God is sovereign."

It would be a statement I would constantly replay in my mind. At the time, they were *just words*. I had no idea of the hope those words represented, and how they would sustain me for years to come.

Going home

Even though it was early Sunday morning, our home was bustling with activity. I love the church family. Without my knowledge and seemingly little mobilization strategy, the boys were being attended to, food was appearing, the house was being cleaned, and folks were visiting. I'll always be grateful for my other families, too. My Brazos Christian School and Texas A&M University families sprang into action doing anything that needed to be done.

If you have lost a loved one, you are well aware of the protocol during those hours that follow death. Calls to close family, calls to dear friends. The most difficult calls were to my parents, who adored Trina and considered her their daughter, and to my brother Bobby, whom Trina loved. But the hardest call was to Trina's brother, Benjamin, whom she cherished. Benjamin is a physician, so explaining the medical part was easy. In fact, he tried to prepare me for the inevitable, but I never could wrap my head around the possibility. But despite Benjamin's training and practice as a surgeon, nothing could have prepared him for this phone call. Trina was his sister—his only sibling. Their dad passed away a few decades prior, and their mom had died of breast cancer in 1983. Now, his sister was gone. As Benjamin and I wept, we tried to encourage each other. All the while I continued to replay Dwight's words, "God is sovereign."

After a full day of making more calls to inform loved ones that Trina had gone home (for years, I could not say the word "dead" in reference to her), my friends Dwight and Haywood suggested I get some sleep. It would be the first of many sleepless nights, where a relentless headache pounded loneliness and despair into my heart. I often reached across the bed to hold Trina, but she wasn't there. I wanted to talk to her. I needed to hear her voice. Suddenly, I felt this overwhelming urge to be with her.

I wanted to go home too.

As more guests arrived and more food appeared, I felt like I was in a trance. I remember speaking, but my words did not make any sense. Here's the best way to describe it: You feel like you're watching a horror movie, only to discover you are actually in the movie.

Other widows and widowers have shared this very same feeling with me. You know it's happening—you just can't believe it's happening to you. Trina was not supposed to die. Mom was not supposed to leave her boys. Nothing, absolutely nothing prepares you for this. Many people have said, "Well, at least you and the boys had time to prepare." But not even five years of uncertainty can prepare you for one second of paralyzing terror. And you can't possibly understand unless it's your spouse, your parent, your sibling, or your child.

Reality has a profoundly clear way of settling in. If Sunday was a time for shock and tears, Monday was a time for the "business" of death. I soon discovered I was not prepared for Monday either.

To initiate the process required to obtain burial benefits, I had to go to the university's System's Office. I was going through the motions of filling out the necessary paperwork, when one section of the application paralyzed me with overwhelming grief. The one-sentence section required a response:

Single ___ Married ___ Divorced ____ Widow____ Widower ____

I selected "Widower," and for the very first time in my life, I felt all alone. I sat at that nice desk in that fancy office and had a major meltdown. I cried uncontrollably, calling Trina's name aloud. I couldn't believe my new identity and I hated it. At age forty, I was no longer a husband. My new identity had become: Rick Rigsby, widower.

It took me about an hour to accomplish what should have taken five minutes. I just couldn't stop staring at that word. Widower. To this day, when I meet a widow or a widower, my heart aches. Just the mention of the word takes me right back to the valley on that morning in September.

A few days later, I remember heading to the funeral home with the clothing she would wear in the casket, and suddenly found myself immersed in the memories of the last time I saw her wearing the dress. The occasion was festive, and Trina looked most lovely. She possessed a casual elegance that reflected a gentle grace and a sincere style.

I allowed my mind to journey back to the first time I saw her in this particular dress—a cream-colored chiffon number that highlighted her perfect figure and coffee-brown skin. She glowed. And that smile!

Every time I saw her smile, it took me back to my college days at Chico State, and October 31, 1974, the night I asked the most beautiful girl I'd ever seen to dance. From the moment she said, "Yes," I lived a fairytale life with my very own princess.

My reminiscing was brought to a sudden halt as we turned into the parking lot of the funeral home. Trina would now wear this dress for a very different occasion.

The funeral

The Franklin family is a wonderful and talented group of people who served as funeral directors for many years in College Station. As a minister who officiated many funeral services, I worked with the

Franklins on numerous occasions. However, this day I was on the other side of the desk. Instead of standing on a mountaintop pulpit citing Psalm 23, I was deep in the valley of the shadow of death.

As the Franklins gently and lovingly suggested the order of the funeral service, I found myself not able to comprehend what was being said. I couldn't process simple information. This was the start of a trend that would take nearly a year to overcome.

When I was a television reporter before graduate school, my job required that I synthesize enormous amounts of information into accurate and brief narratives. Sitting in that funeral home, I was unable to track a conversation or construct a simple declarative statement for a response.

My heart was beating and I was breathing, but I wasn't functioning. I could feel myself shutting down. And now, instead of talking about Jeremiah's basketball game or Andrew's birthday party, we were discussing visitations and choice of caskets.

I felt like crawling into a casket and staying there.

I recall having to surrender Trina's clothing while struggling with my wife being in the funeral home's prep room. Theologically, I knew Trina was not there. But a widower of two days doesn't think logically, or theologically for that matter.

The viewing was even worse. With each step toward Trina's casket, I fought a relentless tirade of emotion that screamed, Turn around! Get out of here! Go home!

At the time, you're not thinking. You want to bolt. Then, you get a glimpse of your boys, dealing with the worst experience a child can endure. Few things in life are as sad as the faces of motherless children. Next, your eyes locate your mother and father. You sense their feeling of helplessness in their inability to take the pain from their son and grandsons. You glance around the room at the profound sadness. And in front you—in repose—a woman in her early forties. Gone.

Mapping the valley

I'm sharing the agonizing details of my story for two reasons.

First, so those of you in the midst of the valley know I've been there and will allow me to deliver a message of hope. And secondly, to help those of you who want to support someone experiencing intense grief.

Most of all, this message will equip you with something I was missing. In fact, this essential element was missing most of my life. My tank was empty, and I could feel it. But I didn't know what I was missing.

When you're in the midst of the valley, it's difficult to see any way out. You can't see your life getting any better any time soon. The words of wonderful, well-intentioned friends bounce off like a rubber ball hitting a wall. You politely smile, but in your heart, you're in the fight of your life.

Consider what one encounters in the midst of trauma:

1. Uncertainty. You're not convinced you're going to survive. For me, suicide was a constant thought, and I fantasized about solutions to end my pain. If not for two boys to raise, I don't even want to imagine where my thoughts would've taken me. Resilience can be the by-product here. For me, that resilience would take years to emerge.

2. Unevenness. You're attempting to adjust to a new normal, only to discover there will never be any such thing as normal. I'll never forget the inescapable paralysis of being "stuck" in the months that followed Trina's death. At this stage, life has moved on for everyone except you and your children.

3. Fear. The future betrayed me. Why should I trust it anymore? My anger and uncertainty masked a frightening new outlook on life. I once looked on the future like a reliable old friend. Now I was afraid of the future—*afraid to hope.*

For me, Rick Rigsby, the most social creature on God's green earth, the party was over. I canceled many opportunities to meet friends for lunch or dinner because I couldn't bear being a "fifth wheel."

What I'm about to say next will make no sense if you're in the deepest part of the valley. But read on anyway.

Two decades removed, I've had much time to reflect on the worst months of my life. And while I wouldn't wish them upon anyone, I state with conviction: Those difficult days shaped my life far more than mountaintop experiences.

In the valley I found what was missing in my life, and in the lives of thousands I've spoken with. But let me not get ahead of myself.

Back to 1996. Life was out of control, and I was about to be.

Chapter 3

MEDICATING
THE PAIN

Truthfully, my life began spiraling downward nearly six years before the funeral—when Trina was diagnosed with breast cancer in 1991.

Our perfectly manicured life was unraveling, as I seemingly lost control of everything: my future, my marriage, and even my daily schedule. The dominoes fell like this: The doctors order chemotherapy and radiation that determines your weekly schedule. Vacations are canceled, outings are postponed, and routines are adjusted. In essence, you lose control over things you took for granted just a month earlier.

If this observation strikes you as selfish on my part, you're way ahead of where I was then. *Oh, poor Rick. His schedule was disrupted.*

But the desire for control is part of human nature. And the emotional reaction to losing control is often a twisted resolve to regain it in any way possible. I still had control over seeking pleasure to numb the pain. And I found pleasure in two things: wallowing in my feelings, and food.

How I felt became the barometer on which I decided everything. If I didn't "feel" like doing something, that was my permission not to do it. If I "felt" as though I should do something, my decision was made.

My feelings became my comfort, protection, and motivation. I fell in love with feelings, and his best friends, comfort and convenience. They all worked to medicate pain by giving me permission to avoid any person, conversation, or situation that I deemed may have the potential to hurt. I vividly recall a luncheon invitation with friends just a month or so after the funeral. I knew I was going to get the constant question, "So, how are you doing?" followed by the proverbial "it's time to move on" pep talk. By using my feelings to avoid the luncheon, I could protect myself from the realities of questions I did not want to answer and shifts and adjustments I was not ready to embrace.

While being led by my feelings was good medicine, food consumption became my primary drug of choice. Nobody could control how often and how much I ate. Food allowed me to medicate myself without the social stigmas usually attached to excessive drinking, taking drugs, or other vices. Few would raise an objection to my drug of choice.

And my prescribed dosage only increased after the funeral.

Seemingly in the blink of an eye, I was widowed, alone, and mad at God. And tipping the scales at over 400 pounds. The excessive weight was the mere outward manifestation of an emotional trauma I refused to acknowledge. Despite being a minister, I was not prepared to deal with grief and grew obsessed with dulling the pain. To ease the pain of Trina's sickness and death, I lusted for food and ate without limit. I became an "emotional" eater. But I was unaware these choices were pushing me to extremes in every area of my life.

Out of bounds

Living on the edge squeezes margin from our lives. And quality of life is found in this margin space—between what we must do and what we want to do. Pastor Andy Stanley is spot on when he states, "Capacity is not determined by how much we have; capacity is determined by our priorities." My top priority became pain management at all cost. It was a priority that minimized my capacity for quality of life: spiritually, mentally, and physically.

From the time of Trina's diagnosis, my first priority was caring for her and our children, followed by dealing with the pain caused by anger and uncertainty. After Trina's passing, medicating my pain became my top priority. My number one focus was to stop hurting—to simply feel nothing—if only for a few minutes.

I convinced myself that the more I could medicate myself with food, the less my heart would ache. My capacity for living life was now based on a need for emotional numbness. At the time, I had no idea my new priorities would cause my life to spiral out of control.

Food became the other woman, my mistress, my sweetheart, the thing I adored most. Like an addict looking for a fix, I longed for food throughout the day. I dreamed about food at night. Simply stated, I *worshiped* food. Pastor and theologian John Piper once stated, "What we hunger for most, we worship."[1]

As a traveling minister and motivational speaker, I've spent countless years traveling from city to city, and fantasizing about favorite dishes at favorite restaurants. Here's a taste.

Hungry? Here we go!

If I was in Atlanta, I had to visit Gladys Knight's *House of Chicken and Waffles*. Jackson, Mississippi, meant *Pinn's Fish House*, featuring delta catfish, with all the trimmings. Hartford, Connecticut, meant the

---

[1] Piper, John. *A Hunger For God*. Wheaton, IL: Good News Publishers, 1997, p. 10.

Italian sausage carbonara at *Carbone's*. In San Francisco, I would devise a plan to visit many of my favorites including *Scoma's* for Seafood Sauté with pasta, sourdough bread, and clam chowder. Then, there's *Pazzia's* on Third Street, where I began with thin-crust pizza and worked my way through a salad, an entrée featuring anything from veal shank to fresh fish, homemade pasta, and dessert. Then there's *Sears International Restaurant*, founded by Ben Sears, a retired circus clown, whose wife Hilbur inherited recipes and opened their place in 1938. Let's not forget *Tadish Grill* on California Street. Or how about a short drive south of the city to the best breakfast ever—*Alana's* in Burlingame where "Martha's Famous Swedish Oatmeal pancakes with Lingonberries" is worth the entire trip.

In Des Moines, Iowa, I'd be planning for a steak at *801 Steakhouse*. In Pittsburgh, I had to have a sandwich from *Primanti Brothers*— famous for cramming the slaw and fries right into the sandwich! In Indianapolis, I planned a visit to *St. Elmo's* for their world-famous shrimp cocktail, followed by a succulent navy bean soup. These dishes were merely the warm-up act to one of the best steaks in America.

Speaking of best steaks in America, whenever I speak in Minneapolis, I would daydream about how soon I could get to *Manny's*—whose steaks are so large they cover the plate. In Chicago, *Mike Ditka's* restaurant is an all-day love affair. I usually begin with pot roast nachos followed by a house salad, and then the largest pork chop in the Midwest. Every trip to anywhere within 100 miles of Kansas City meant a visit to either *Jack's Stack*, *Arthur Bryant's*, or *Oklahoma Joe's*. The KC BBQ is so good it would make a vegetarian consider backsliding!

Whether it's lemon chicken at *Rao's* New York, or Bobby Flay's *Mesa Grill* in Las Vegas, or ribs and baked potato salad at the *Whole Hog* in Little Rock, or a second helping of pancakes smothered with macadamia sauce at *Boots and Kimo's* in Kailua, Hawaii, or Cuban cuisine at *Columbia* in Tampa Bay, I became spellbound by the chase, capture, and consumption of food.

This is the way I lived <u>every day</u> for decades. I know why they call it "comfort food." I was comforting myself and medicating my pain without breaking any laws. And nobody was going to control me or tell me how much or how little I could eat. I was in complete control.

A lifelong love affair

As a child, being escorted to the "husky" section of the J. C. Penney department store was a small price to pay for eating an endless supply of Hostess cupcakes and fruit pies. Being laughed at and called "chubby" was painful—until I realized if I made others laugh, they'd laugh with me and not at me.

My parents were the absolute best. And while we had little, one thing was certain—my brother and I never went hungry one day in our lives. My father and mother—from Texas and Oklahoma respectively—were children of the Depression. I recall them reminiscing about their childhood, often saying, "If our parents didn't catch it, shoot it, grow it, pickle it, can it, or preserve it, we learned how to do without it."

By the time we children came along in the 50s and early 60s, my parents demonstrated their love by providing for us. This translated to Sunday feasts, typically featuring two types of meats and an array of scrumptious sides.

There was a time in my mid-twenties when I went on a "health kick" for a few weeks. Mother and Daddy were visiting and I decided to prove a point by serving soup and salad. My father was very polite during dinner, but not so much afterward. Waiting for a moment when we were alone, he said, "Son, don't ever serve us soup and salad. If you need some money for food, just ask us."

For my parents—and for that matter, for many of their generation—providing a roof over your head, clothes on your back, and plenty of food on the table meant you had succeeded in life. It communicated that no matter how tough times were, you had provided for your family. And so, we learned early on to eat in abundance. There would be no limits placed upon our eating. Eating became a pillar of our existence, the stability that grounded our family, and the symbolism of celebration for every occasion.

Looking in the mirror

The restaurants I mentioned are extraordinary and continue to be among my favorites. And my story about Mother and Daddy is no condemnation on my parents. I had the best childhood imaginable, where breakfast, lunch, and dinner were enchanting culinary masterpieces. My mealtime memories are not only about food, but of animated conversations and unrestrained laughter, squeezed in between each delectable bite! For me, mealtime was a celebration, something that even as a child I would long for.

My parents provided not only food and shelter, but also the emotional stability necessary for our well-being. Daddy said his goal was to rear men—not boys. We learned from our father how to be men of courage and conviction. My mother reminded us—seemingly every day—that we were destined for greatness. She asserted rather forcefully that we would accomplish much, and could achieve anything we set our minds to.

My brother—who is a respected Superior Court judge in Washington, D.C., and a retired Colonel in the United States Army— would agree that the success we both have achieved is the direct result of the firm foundation established by our parents.

As a child, I overate because it was the norm, and there were no limitations enforced. Our parents saw a primary responsibility to put a roof over our heads and food in our stomachs. For our family, food was not simply fuel. Food was the way our parents showed their love for and commitment to us. After college, in my job as an on-air television news reporter, I had to offer a reasonably decent appearance. While always overweight, I spent my twenties and thirties "in range" of good health. I was six feet tall, weighed about 250 pounds, and was motivated to maintain that weight not because of health concerns, but based on how I would appear on TV.

Looks can be deceiving.

Inside out

My best friend, Haywood Robinson, was very worried about me. He wasn't just my friend but my doctor as well. I was a mess physically, emotionally, and socially. I was the most outgoing person God ever created. And suddenly, I lost all motivation to do or go or be. In fact, I remember Haywood saying he had not seen me smile in months. I had gone from being *the life of the party* to avoiding the party.

So, in an effort to help, Haywood and his wife Noreen and daughters Udelle and Riva decided the boys and I needed to join them on a cruise. A cruise, they said, is what would bring me out of my funk. My boys loved the idea. I wasn't so sure. I did not want to have fun or make any efforts to interact with strangers. I just wanted to be. However, that cruise proved to be just the thing I needed.

The first thing I realized is that while Trina had died, and I thought I had too, some part of me was still alive. For the first time since Trina had passed away nine months earlier, I was laughing and joking and joyful.

I remember my best day of the cruise. It would also turn out to be my worst day.

I wandered into a jewelry store during an on-shore excursion in the Cayman Islands. I spotted this beautiful ring, and suddenly, made a very strange decision to buy the new ring for my right hand. I really could not afford to buy such an expensive ring, but that didn't stop me. I was on top of the world. I was laughing again and felt joyful, a feeling I had not experienced in a long time. Spending money had done much more than take my mind off things; it gave me a sense of hope.

My life was about to get better. And my new ring would symbolize that turning point.

I bought the ring at 3:00 p.m. The cruise ship departed at 6:00 p.m., and I was the life of the party—dancing and enjoying the festivities with my new ring—which represented a new life. Then, strange decision number two. I took off my wedding ring for the first time since Trina passed. *Why wear a wedding ring reminding me of what I lost, when I can wear a celebration ring of new things to come?*

By 10:00 p.m. that night, I was alone in the cabin I shared with the boys. Drowning in my own tears, I yanked the new ring off and tenderly slipped my wedding ring back on. Less than eight hours of "hope" cost me $4,000, and set me back emotionally six months.

False hope is delusional—and costly. As the old Miller Lite beer commercial stated, "It tastes great, but it's less filling." This is the perfect summation for false hope. I've had two decades to think about the events of that day which led to me buy a ring. Allow me to detail my thoughts and feelings in numerical sequence:

1. *You really don't desire to have fun.*
2. *You find yourself having fun.*
3. *Maybe it's time to get on with your life.*

4. *But pain and loneliness have become special friends.*

5. *Something inside wants to move on.*

6. *Something inside wants to stay in control.*

7. *I can accomplish moving on and control with a purchase.*

8. *No one is ever going to tell me what I must do anymore.*

9. *And I deserve to live and deserve to move on.*

10. *In fact, I don't need to even justify this purchase to myself.*

As you note the progression of thought, you see a hurting person who isn't dealing with his pain in a healthy way. Furthermore, you see a person who's out of control but desperately wants to be in control. Most of all, you see a person who wants to hope but is *afraid to hope* in an authentic way. Instead, the thought of false hope becomes appealing and, for a time, less costly.

A quick fix

I want you to note the sheer hopelessness in my thought processes. I sought a fix—immediate medication to relieve my pain. It's actually no different than a junkie needing drugs, or an alcoholic needing a drink, something I discovered by counseling folks in a pastoral role.

Here's the bottom line. More important than logic or wisdom or even common sense, in the heart of someone in the valley, is this surging impulse to find immediate relief. The question I've asked myself for 20 years is, *why?* My answer: I saw no hope.

And in the absence of hope, you create your own imitation. Wisdom, logic, budget, and caloric intake or carbs consumed become the least of your concerns. But let me caution you, a "quick fix" is not a fix, and there's nothing quick about it. You wake up asking what so many of us have asked after our own lapses: *Dear God, what have I done?'*

Here's my question for you: What's *your* ring? What's your quick fix?

Right now, stop reading, close this book, and ask yourself, *Am I just medicating my pain? Is my "ring" merely false hope?*

Filling the void

Life was out of control. When Trina and I received her life-changing diagnosis, my hunger for control went into overdrive. I masked my pain with feelings and food. It took me years to realize I was spiritually malnourished and emotionally bankrupt. I was empty inside, and 400 pounds outside.

Through the years I heard hundreds, maybe thousands, of well-meaning condolences and beautiful encouragements. But for months following Trina's death, Dwight's simple statement still haunted me. I sensed something strangely helpful and true in those words. "Rick, I don't know why Trina died, but I know God is sovereign." Embedded in those words was the ingredient I was missing, the essential element for the life I craved.

My expectation for the future was listlessly passive. Life was supposed to just happen, and happen well. When it didn't, I was caught unprepared and unequipped.

I had no hope.

Whatever hope I had as a child and young man was woefully replaced with resignation and low expectation. I created idols for myself. I created false hope—cheap imitations of hope—all centered around me and my desires. The issue wasn't just a plate of nachos. It was having the ability to control when I took the drug and how much of the drug I wanted to take.

My whole day, and much of the preceding week, was structured around chasing a food fix and being led by my feelings.

More pain. More medication.

Less hope. More false hope.

Now that I understand what hope truly is, I can say there has never been less of it in the world. We're starving for hope—and it shows.

Looking forward, looking back

In recent years, I've asked myself, *What kind of choices could I have made that would have stopped my downward spiral?*

My answer may surprise you.

Chapter 4

BUYING REAL ESTATE IN THE VALLEY

Nothing is as attractive as the promise of hope.

Nothing is as life changing as the motivation of hope.

Nothing is as transformational as a heart filled with hope.

Because hope—real hope—is so uncommon and so rarely offered, it stands out.

Do you prefer to be around a downer kind of person or a hopeful person? Would you rather do business with a hope-filled person or a person who thinks the sky is falling?

Never become friends with someone because you agree with them on negatives. Find friends whom you agree with on positives, which is to say you both share a common hope.

Nothing is as attractive as the possibility of hope. Nothing is as life changing as the motivation of hope. Nothing is more transformative than a heart filled with hope.

What if?

Do you detest *what if* questions? Me, too. I used to anyway.

When I was in the valley, if you said to me, "Imagine God using your hopeless situation to bring hope into thousands and thousands of lives," I would have had several reactions.

Number one, I wouldn't have believed you.

Number two, I would've held on to those words for dear life.

My mind may have dismissed you, and my emotions might've become enraged by your insensitivity. But my heart would have wrapped itself around the seed of hope in those words.

In the valley, I received many gifts from wonderful people: groceries, meals, beautiful cards, and flowers. But other than my two friends Dwight Edwards and Haywood Robinson, I received very little hope. Instead of buying a sympathy card—and by the way, most grieving people I know hate sympathy cards—what if you planted a seed of hope?

But before you go around trying to be an ambassador of hope you must, I repeat, you *must* let hope transform *you* from the inside out. In other words, read on, friend. In a generation of quick fixes and fast remedies, I'm not entirely sure we know what's really meant by the term "hope."

I know how you feel

People who are grieving hear a lot of well-intentioned words and well wishes. You might be surprised to learn that most of them—regardless of how sincerely offered—miss the mark.

Consider a few of the common expressions shared with someone who has lost a spouse. (The following list continues to cut deeply to this day, which is why I share my commentary on each.). As you read, ask yourself, *do any of these expressions contain hope?*

Rick, I know just how you feel. My grandfather passed away last summer.

(Keep in mind, my wife was 41 years of age when she passed.)

Rick, I can really sympathize with you. We lost our family dog last month.

(Don't get me wrong. I'm a dog lover and dog owner, too. But this was my wife.)

Rick, I know you're lonely, but she's in a better place now.

(Yes, I'm well aware her spirit is with Jesus. But I want her with us!)

Rick, don't worry. You'll get another wife to replace her.

(So absurd, no commentary needed.)

Rick, I know just how you feel. My grandmother had breast cancer. Scared us for a while, but she's doing much better now.

Did you find any hope in any of those statements? I certainly did not. It's almost as if the statement helped them more than me. I noted that people—sincere in their efforts—looked for some way to connect with your pain. Their hearts were right, but their words were misguided. Friend, when you encounter a grieving person, please refrain from beginning a sentence with, *I know just how you feel.* You don't. I don't even have an idea how another widower might feel. Sure, there are some similarities, but grief is uniquely experienced.

I would smile, nod in the affirmative, and say little. I realized that sincere people were trying to help by offering words they thought might uplift. They did not.

The following represents what I really wanted to say to people:

I lost my best friend, my soulmate, my lover, the mother of my children, the woman I was to grow old with. My boys miss their mom. I worry day and night whether they'll be damaged for life. I see the pain on their faces and I cannot take it away. I am empty, lonely, heartbroken, devastated, depressed, despondent, disillusioned, distracted, doubtful, and in denial. I'm on an emotional roller coaster at an amusement park that never closes. You walk away from me and hold hands with your spouse. I return to an empty house. You awake and go about your business. I stay up all night crying, crawl out of bed with a throbbing headache, and try to figure out how to avoid the reality of another horrible, hopeless day.

You have no idea how I feel! And, how dare you assume you do!

I write about this less as a critique, and more as how to engage with people going through grief. Talk less, listen more. And, if they don't want to talk, that's fine too. Often, just having someone near and feeling their presence was reassuring.

I remember one phrase that stung severely. While greeting friends at the repast following the funeral, a man walked up to me and said, "Trina belongs to us all now."

I wanted to punch him in the face.

These words may not seem like such a big deal, but she was *my* wife, not yours! She was *my* boys' mom, not yours! I'm sure to this day, the man had no clue how little hope or encouragement he offered. It would take me years to forgive him, and so many others. But at the time, I just shook my head in agreement and buried the rage.

Over the years, I've heard people say unbelievable things. On a few occasions, I've witnessed someone comment to a grieving parent, "God will give another one to replace the child you lost." People are not replaceable.

I've even had several people tell me, "Rick, at least you had nearly six years to prepare for Trina's passing." First, you don't spend every day planning for your wife to die. You couldn't possibly live that way. Secondly, nothing prepares you for a doctor coming out of an emergency room, lowering his head and saying, "I'm sorry."

Let me say again, I share these insights not because I'm angry now, but because I want us to become real encouragers—agents of genuine hope. Our words will either stir anger, hurt, and desperation—or encourage the healing process and give people tremendous hope. I would have to remind myself that people are well intentioned, sincere, and often ignorant. So was I. Trust me, before the valley I'd say anything that came to mind to a grieving person. And, I was okay with that because my heart was in the right place. Your heart may be in the right place, but your choice of words can be so devastating it becomes impossible to see your motivation.

The Roman philosopher Cicero once stated that eloquent rhetoric (communication) is "the graceful arrangement of words."[2] The Bible says, "Let your speech be always with grace" (Colossians 4: 6 KJV). The reference indicates the term *grace* is applied as an additive (like salt as a seasoning) to elevate speech to honorable and right rather than meaningless and trite.

Sometimes the most helpful words are unspoken.

Silence

Do you want to help a friend who's in a valley? Just be there. Don't say a word. Here's how I learned this, although I must admit I didn't realize the profound lesson at the time.

---

[2] Marcus Tullius Cicero. De Oratore, (55 BCE). In, *De Oratore in Cicero Rhetorica*. Vol. I (*De Oratore*). Edited by A. S. Wilkins. Clarendon Press Oxford Classical Texts 264 pages. ISBN 978-0-19-814615-5, (March 1963).

You recall that I mentioned my friend and doctor, Haywood Robinson? His mother—Mama Robinson—who cared for Trina, would come over and help us in the months following Trina's death. Mama would come during the daytime. But the nights were most difficult. Haywood spent many evenings with me in 1996, several of those were when *Monday Night Football* was on. We would watch TV together, but the television was never on. I would cry and he would just sit. What I'm saying is this: Your words may not make a quantifiable change in a person's life. However, your presence always will.

If you believe this world needs more hope, we must educate ourselves about what true hope is. Otherwise, at a person's most vulnerable moment in life, we'll offer shallow, trite, and meaningless sentiments that give little comfort and even less hope.

Hope is different

The day following Trina's Texas funeral, we celebrated our son, Jeremiah's birthday—a wonderful diversion. The next morning, we flew to Northern California for a second service in Chico, the town where we met, went to college, and lived for nearly two decades. Again, family and friends gave tremendous support and love.

Regardless, what began with the first "I'm sorry," from the doctor turned into a chorus of, "I'm so sorry" and lasted several months. And, while I sincerely appreciate every single expression and word of sympathy, Haywood's presence and Dwight's parking lot comment were the only expressions that offered me any hope.

To refresh your memory, Dwight—just hours after Trina was pronounced dead—said, "Rick, I don't know why Trina died, but I know God is sovereign." Sometime later, I would reflect on the word, "but" and noted how it knocked the wind out of my self-absorption and pointed to another path. While my mind was spinning, that one word placed a demand on my spirit. His was the only comment that contained a "but." And the concept was disruptive to say the least.

What was the big deal about Dwight's comment? All he did was introduce the *possibility* of hope that God is in control. Just the possibility. Just for one minute. I have always believed that God is for us, and that His plans are for our good. This belief was challenging my sense of hopelessness.

Mixed in with the *sorry*'s were some, "Just wait and see how the Lord's going to use you," which sounds a lot like hope. But it's not. Do you know why? Because it was about me. Well-meaning comments like this turned the attention back to me, and that's exactly what I didn't need. Also, when a person is in the valley, they *need* help. The last thing on my mind was *giving* help. Also, a statement that begins with, "just wait," is actually "hope deferred." And, I am a firm believer that "hope deferred makes the heart sick..." (Proverbs 13:12).

One of my sensitive spots was when I perceived people attempting to check me off that day's "to do" list, or offer a quick word so they could appear compassionate and move on. When you think about it, the phrase "just wait" absolves the person from dealing with the moment and reassures them there will be no awkward moments. But here's the deal: It *is* awkward talking with someone who's grieving. Most say things that don't help and offer little hope. To this day, I hate the line, "just wait." Such a statement begs the question, "What about now?" Now—right now—right in the midst of this valley is when I need hope. And you're suggesting that I continue waiting?

Dwight's statement was so profound because it shifted my attention off me and caused me to wonder if I could trust God—if only for a moment. I loved God. I just didn't know if I could trust Him.

Again, I've been on the giving end of some beautifully hurtful sentiments and wonderfully misguided condolences. I've sent the sympathy card and checked the grieving person off my to-do list, when I could've been an agent of hope. It was all about me.

I remember a very sad day—about a month after Trina's death. Amidst my tears, I am listening to radio preacher Charles Stanley's *In Touch* show. At the conclusion of the show, the announcer encouraged those suffering to call the 800 number for prayer. My five-minute prayer lasted forty-five minutes as a grieving widower connected with an angel who simply listened. I remember the prayer partner seemed so helpless but she was so compassionate. The only reason I called was to satisfy my insatiable search for hope. Still no luck. But, I learned a valuable lesson. The person listened and said very little. In other words, she never made the call about her. That was never my experience as I eagerly shared advice with those grieving.

Clearly now, I see the need for authenticity, and sometimes it comes in the form of silence—sacrificing your agenda for the sake of genuinely encouraging another.

For the moment

If you're hurting, and if you don't understand what hope really is, you'll be stuck without seeing any relief. I originally learned this as a chaplain for the Texas A&M football team. When you're in the middle of two-a-day practices in the sweltering summer heat of Texas, it can be a challenge to remember the big picture. The big picture is: You cannot enjoy the victories on the mountaintop, without facing and overcoming perceived losses in the valley. Those valley challenges often are most disruptive. But ask any successful entrepreneur and they'll confirm you won't experience success without disruption. That same success principle applies to college football.

A rigorous Division I season awaits, and in the back of a player's mind he knows the work must be put in to weather the storm of a demanding season. But on some of those summer days during Texas A&M football's training camp, I found it very difficult to convince players to keep the big picture in mind in the midst of the battle. You have to remind them that it's what a warrior must do.

It wasn't until we were in the midst of an intensely grueling season that I'd hear players exclaim, "That's why we did all that work in the off season!" Rarely is that comment echoed while *in* the valley. But in the valley, in the pain, we have the sensational desire to simply numb the pain. It's natural. And let's be clear. The situation is *not* good. The situation is bad. You're still going to deal with the grief. You're still going to deal with the anger. But God has a way of finding some good in it.

We survived

I've spoken with many people heartbroken from divorce. Those who learned hope the hard way, or the easy way, have told me this: "Oh, but I found myself. I discovered things about myself I would've never discovered before. I have a new life." No matter what you're going through, or will face in the future, what if massive amounts of good can come from the experience? Consider this statement that I have made for the last several years:

How could the worst thing that ever happened to me be the best thing?

My friend and best-selling author John Mason asks a similar question, "How many of you have survived the worst thing that's ever happened to you?" Yeah, it's okay to laugh, or breathe a sigh of relief. Because we *have* survived.

Following my speeches or sermons, I have the honor of speaking with many people who are reeling from the loss of a spouse. When they say, "For me it was two years ago" or "For me it was twenty years ago," I'll say two simple words: "We survived." And we hug. And maybe even cry. That's putting hands and feet on hope.

We survived. Those are loaded words. We know they mean: *We could've taken ourselves out. We should be in the mental institution. We might've lost our way. We could've abandoned God. We should've checked out. But … we survived.*

Hopeful words remind people of the hope that's already in them. That's what my calling is in life. My calling is to give people hope. And how do I do that? By reminding them hope already exists in them. Even for a few seconds, hope can help us change course. Instead of buying a home in the valley, I began to imagine moving to a better place.

Swimming in a sea of negativity

Based on the conversations I hear, and based on the conversations in the media, most people find it easier to complain as opposed to being agents of hope.

You know what flight attendants tell me after almost every flight? No, it's not, "Sorry sir, you can't have another Diet Coke for the road." They'll say, "You're the nicest passenger we've had in a while." But that's not a compliment to me. That's an indictment of our culture and the swirling winds of negativity that surround us.

I've had flight attendants tell me, "Sir, thank you for taking your headphones off when I serve you. Most people just look down." Why am I talking about common courtesy in the unfriendly skies? Because it speaks to the absence of hope in our society on a fundamental level. It's affected our creativity. It's affected how we treat one another. It's affecting every aspect of our lives.

Here's how I put hands and feet on hope in a very simple way: I make sure I smile at flight attendants and restaurant employees. I make sure I ask them how their day is going. I seek out older people and show honor to them. Instead of trying to impress you, by being the first one on the plane, I purposely look for older people with bags and see if I can help them to their seat.

"That restores my hope in humanity." How many times have we had this reaction to kindness? But doesn't this mean most of us are walking around without hope? We've lost the basics of living because we've lost the basics of hope.

The basics of the essential

My father was a cook at California Maritime Academy in Northern California. Though he was *just* a galley staffer, he was the wisest man I have ever met. He always said, "Son, in every restaurant you go to, taste the soup. If the soup isn't good, don't invest in the restaurant."

I'm reminded of legendary UCLA basketball coach John Wooden and the first lesson he taught his players: the proper way to put on socks. His logic was if you don't put socks on properly, your feet develop blisters and you're no good to the team.

Before my friend, Dwight Edwards, was a pastor, author, and speaker, he was a professional tennis player in the 1970s. I once asked Dwight who was his toughest competition. Thinking he'd say Jimmy Connors or Arthur Ashe, Dwight offered up Bjorn Borg. Dwight said that Borg had so mastered the fundamentals he simply wore down his opponents.

In each of these three illustrations, you see one common denominator: Mastering the basics is key to improvement. How would the quality of our lives be affected if we understood—and practiced—the basics regardless of the present situation? I recall reading where former NFL coach Chuck Knoll said on one occasion, "Champions are champions not because they do extraordinary things, but because they do ordinary things better than anyone else."

My valley experience was defined by three words: All. About. Me. And those three words keep us from receiving hope—and keep us from giving hope to others. How can you be an agent of hope if it's all about you?

But, Rick, I'm hurting. It is all about me right now, isn't it?

Certainly, I'm not advocating against taking care of yourself and taking time to heal. But part of the cure for getting unstuck is getting our eyes off ourselves. This might sound impossible, but trust me.

One of the most profound lessons my mother and father ever taught me was to make sure my servant's towel was bigger than my ego.

Ego is the anesthesia that deadens the pain of stupidity.

My dad was very proud of my television career. But he was also wise enough to know how that kind of environment could elevate one's ego. When I would talk to my dad, he would help me deal with that ego by reminding me to make sure my servant's towel was bigger than my ego.

We're so narcissistic that even our Facebook pictures don't look like us.

Serving other people forces you to remove the shackles of your own sense of self-importance. You can't serve others when it's all about you.

Today's leadership model, in business and church, says we need to be about the business of cross-functional teams where we're making leaders of everyone. So, here's an interesting question for leaders: Are you willing to forego your place of preeminence to allow another to be preeminent?

Even during intense pain and grief, could selfishness be why we're not practicing the basics of hope? The mantras of "What about me?" or "Why me?" will only keep us stuck. Because we're so injured, we can't see anything but our struggle. There is wisdom available, if you'll entertain the possibility that the struggle really isn't about you. You're in the struggle but the struggle has a bigger purpose.

You and I are on the unnecessarily-necessary journey from doubt and fear to hope and trust. I settled for false hope because it was cheap and easy. Genuine hope, the hope that forces you to go beyond what you can imagine is costly. And frankly, I was afraid of that kind of hope.

The beauty of the valley

There's lots of false teaching on faith today. I have friends who say, "If you have faith, you won't go through a valley." If this is true, a whole lot of Bible stories need to be rewritten. Let's be honest, we can't see the beauty of the valley if we are paralyzed with fear of the valley. No one wants to be in the valley, but don't we all want to see something good come from the trip?

Your absolute best can come out of you from a valley experience. Why is it that NFL teams say their best progress every year is between week one and week two? What is it that causes a team to go into the World Series on a Thursday night, lose 6-0, then bounce back and win on the last night?

There is something marvelously dynamic waiting to be discovered in the valley. That's the picture I want you to see. Something good is at work whether you acknowledge it or not. So why not take advantage of the potential of being in the valley?

So, pause. Breathe. You're alive.

Could the potential for true greatness be incubating inside you? The answer is yes. You're in the only place where the basics of hope are developed.

Hope is rare

Listen to people talk today. People don't even talk about hope.

But go back a couple of generations. My grandparents hoped for a better life. My mother and father hoped for a better life. They *expected* a better life for their children. I don't know if we've lost our hope as much as we've misplaced it. Hope can seem very transient. When we need it, we grab for it like a feather in the wind. That's because most people can't even define the word. Can you?

Yes, hope is rare. But hope is available in endless supply.

In a society where gratifications are instant and communication is even faster, the illusion becomes quite simple: We get it when we need it and we get it fast because we don't have time to waste. We have ripped the valley experience from the equation of success. Companies don't talk about failure in a positive way. People don't discuss the virtues of setbacks at cocktail parties.

Yet, a growing field of study is emphasizing failure as a catalyst for success.

John Maxwell, in his New York Times best seller, *Failing Forward,* makes the argument: "The difference between average people and achieving people is their perception of and response to failure."[3]

One of my regular reads is *Success* magazine. A bonus for readers is an audio CD included in every monthly issue. In the February 2013

---

[3] John C. Maxwell. *Failing Forward: Turning Mistakes into Stepping Stones for Success.* (Nashville: Thomas Nelson Publishers, 2000), p. 2.

CD edition, I was intrigued by publisher Darren Hardy's take on failure as a catalyst for success. Hardy then told the story of writer J. K. Rowling, the creator of the *Harry Potter* Empire, and how her "hopeless" situation became the inspiration for her success.

Rejected by twelve publishers, Rowling's first Harry Potter book was published in 1995. In her 2008 Harvard University commencement speech titled, "The Fringe Benefits of Failure," Rowling walked graduates through her rags to riches story—from being a penniless, divorced, single mom, to one of the greatest novelists in history:

"Failure meant a stripping away of the nonessential. I stopped pretending to myself that I was anything other than what I was, and began to direct all my energy into finishing the only work that mattered to me. Had I really succeeded at anything else, I might never have found the determination to succeed in the one arena where I believed I truly belonged. I was set free, because my greatest fear had been realized, and I was still alive, and I still had a daughter whom I adored, and I had an old typewriter and a big idea. And so rock bottom became the solid foundation on which I rebuilt my life."[4]

A broken marriage. On state assistance. A single mother. Writing in coffee houses while her daughter slept.

How do you go from *that* valley to *Forbes* magazine estimating your net worth of one billion dollars?

The same way you move from hopelessness to hope: Rock bottom becomes your solid foundation for rebuilding.

---

[4] As one who has listened to and presented countless graduation speeches, Rowling's commencement address is among the best I have ever heard. To view the complete speech, access: J. K. Rowling, Harvard Commencement Speech, June 5, 2008, or connect to the following link: https://www.youtube.com/watch?v=wHGqp8lz36c

Chapter 5

DEMANDING HOPE

As I was writing this book, I decided to ask people how they defined hope. So, I asked people, in very casual settings, to help me understand how they view the term hope. Sometimes, it was a cab driver, other times a clerk at the grocery store checkout. In virtually every encounter, the response had the same tone.

One morning while having breakfast in Tulsa, Oklahoma, I asked my waitperson what hope was. She sighed, "I just hope I can get through the day," and then began telling me about the myriad of challenges she faced. Later that day I asked someone else. She said, "Well, I hope my kids will not see World War III. When I look at my kids, I have hope for the future."

The following responses summarize several months of asking people to define hope:

1. I hope I get good grades
2. I hope my house doesn't flood
3. I hope my car doesn't break down
4. I hope we can stay together forever
5. I hope I can leave this job
6. I hope I get into college

7. I hope we don't go to war

8. I hope I find my phone

9. I hope church gets out early

10. I hope we're having something good for dinner

11. I hope the lines at the post office are not long

12. I hope I get a car for Christmas

How do you define hope?

After asking hundreds of people throughout the country, here's my conclusion. We've done a horrible job defining hope. Hope has been reduced to nothing more than a wish we desire to be fulfilled. Most definitions I've heard boil down to this: Hope is nothing more than a pragmatic addendum—and a transient emotion. A wish. Hope is a feeling that sometimes finds us. It comes and it goes.

Is this all there is?

Are you satisfied with these ethereal definitions of hope?

Me neither. After all, hope is a word we use almost daily. "I hope my team wins." "Let's hope so." "We hope it doesn't rain."

But is there any substance, any backbone, in those words?

Hope is also a cornerstone of the Christian faith.

In the Christian faith, we believe Jesus is the hope of the world, "In his name the nations will put their hope" (Matthew 12:21).

Think about this for a moment. We aren't saying:

* *Jesus is the feel good story for the world.*

* *Jesus is the temporal feeling for the world.*

* *Jesus is the emotional crutch for the world.*

If Christians in fact believe Jesus is the HOPE for the world, then did biblical writers mean more than a fleeting wish or urgent surge of emotion when they were describing the Messiah?

When I read, "The nations will put their hope in Jesus," the presupposition suggests more than a passive, transient *wish*. If the writers of Scripture are arguing that *Jesus is the hope of the world*, is there not more to the word hope than we've been led to believe?

In our present age, we view hope as something wished for. However, the Greek definition of hope is:

"A strong and confident expectation."

Strong's Concordance goes a step further by stating that hope is: an anticipated "expectation of what is certain."[5]

These definitions show the biblical meaning offers a much more powerful—even transformative—definition of hope than the ones we currently embrace or exercise. I can't fully explain why we've lost the meaning of hope or why we've diluted the definition of the word. But I know two things: I was afraid to truly hope, and we all need to recapture the power of hope.

My definition of hope

*Hope is a quality of every human spirit that places
a transformative demand upon our heart to believe
for the absolute best outcome.*

My definition of hope conveys something far more powerful and potent than *hoping* it doesn't rain today. Let's take some time and

---

[5] Strong, James. *Strong's Exhaustive Concordance of the Bible* (Abingdon Press, 1890).

examine the unique properties that distinguish this definition from how we traditionally view hope.

Hope as a quality

To examine the behavior of a toddler is simply wondrous. This age represents the purest form of our human existence. As a toddler, the child hasn't learned to hate, doesn't want revenge, and isn't judgmental. They live in a state of hopeful bliss, whereby they see nothing else but to believe in the best possible outcome. Toddlers expect to be cared for, loved, and admired. Anything less than the expectation produces tears and a facial expression of genuine disbelief. The child knows no other way. They were born to expect a positive outcome.

Hope may produce feelings, but it isn't a feeling. It's a quality, a facet of every human spirit. In other words, whether you realize it or not, you have hope inside you. *You got it. All the time.* The quality of hope has resided inside you from the moment you took your first breath. And just because we're taught or encouraged to minimize or diminish this quality doesn't mean it's nonexistent.

Hope as transformative

What would happen, if for a moment today, we dared to imagine? What would happen if we dared to dream? Regardless of the outcome—whether or not the intended goal is achieved—what happens to the human heart when we shift from hopelessness to what if?

Hoping for a better outcome has transformative power. Daring to dream about a better outcome forces one, for a moment, to embrace different realities and possibilities. These are powerful thoughts that keep and create expectations regardless of the circumstances. The power of such thoughts and their impact upon the heart can't be minimized.

Hope as a choice

Implied in my definition of hope is the notion that we have a choice to decide whether we're going to remain in our current state, or try something different. Choice is powerful. Each day, we choose to be in a bad or good mood. Circumstances aside, we make choices to react in certain ways. I've heard it stated it's not what happens to you, but how you choose to react.

And since you got it, you can choose it. (Just like I can make a choice to use proper grammar or not!)

Hope is standard operating equipment in your spirit.

Have you ever discovered a new feature on your car? And don't even get me started about my phone and computer. I may have a Ph.D., but my washing machine is smarter than me.

Once we unlock a feature, we can make a demand on it and choose to operate it.

Hope resides

My mother and father reared us in a 1,200 square foot home in Northern California. They bought the home for $14,000 in 1954. After my father passed away in 1997, we tried to convince my mother to sell the house, but she didn't want to. She was a Great Depression and World War II survivor who moved from Oklahoma to escape the dust bowl. After she was convinced to sell the house, she was astounded by how much it had appreciated. The sale of the home made enough money to clear her debt, allowed her to travel in her final years, and she was able to leave an inheritance to her family. She could have died not knowing her financial worth. She almost missed out on so much, simply because she didn't know her true financial potential.

The home she resided in had massive potential, which was untapped until she made a demand on it. Your spirit has massive potential for hope. But if you're uninformed, you'll never see the potential. And if you don't see the potential, you'll never make a demand on the wealth of hope that's yours.

What if hope is a "feature" we only imagined, but didn't know was available, or haven't yet understood how to operate? And if hope isn't a mysterious alignment of the planets, but a choice to tap into inside us, we can make a demand on hope every day.

Now that you know hope resides in you, will you make a choice to truly hope?

Every one of us can make an intentional demand on our mind and heart as we deal with problems and pain. How does a true definition of hope affect your anxiety about circumstances out of your control? Those circumstances may still be out of your control, but your ability to cope at a higher level is well within you.

Yes, I'm giving you permission to make an intentional choice to hope. Not when you feel like it, but every day. In fact, that's what makes hope transformative. It can pull us out of the valley and help us pull others out with us.

Hope might not come naturally to your brain. But hope is the best news your brain has heard all day.

Choosing hope places a creative demand on your mind and heart. Here's an example. Your birthday is coming up. What would you like to have for dinner?

Before I asked, you weren't thinking about your birthday dinner, but now you are. (Me, too.) Your mind and heart have a God-given capacity to "see" what you're hoping for: the best possible outcome for your meal.

This example is Hope 101—or kindergarten. But you get the point.

Permission

For most people hope is simply dormant. And when first awakened, hope can feel a bit scary.

Start with this: *I give myself permission to hope.* You are giving yourself permission to consider the possibility of something better.

In the valley, I had to give myself permission to laugh. I had to give myself permission to love. I had to give myself permission to go through a day without fearing one of my kids would die. I had to give myself permission to dare to dream again.

Over time, I began thinking what months earlier seemed impossible to consider: *I wonder if I'll ever fall in love again?* Where in the world did *that* thought come from? And what might Trina think about it?

The thought was released when I gave myself permission to dream again. As for Trina, despite my guilt, she was applauding from heaven. Hard to believe? Consider one of our last conversations captured in this statement: "Ricky, you need to remarry, and I want our boys to have a mom. You were not meant to live alone."

Let's unpack the idea of permission.

Why give yourself permission? Permission is defined as giving consent or authorization to do something. After Trina died, I made a choice not to laugh or to feel joy. That choice was based on my emotions and the feelings of sorrow in my heart. Months, even years later, the sorrow remains in my heart. The reality is—part of me died in 1996. However, I did not die. And in order to live again, my mind must authorize my will to move forward.

My mind must authorize my will to move forward.

Nothing inside of me wanted to move forward. Everything inside of me wanted to continue being motivated by what I was feeling. This incongruent thinking creates a crisis of the spirit—either you're going to move on, or you're not. Everyone reaches this fork in the path of life, perhaps many times throughout our lives. I had to give myself permission to move forward. I had to give myself permission to laugh, to love, to take a chance, to live.

This is where we start. Give ourselves permission to hope. Every day.

Puddles

Back to my conversation with the waitperson, while researching the question of hope for this book, as she concluded she wondered out loud, "When did I stop hoping?"

Without thinking, I said, "Probably the day you stopped skipping."

We both agreed to study our younger family members—me, my grandchildren eight and five at the time—the waitperson, her kids. Why study them? Just look at the behavior of children. They laugh. They run. They jump. They play. They dream. They skip. They don't walk around puddles; they walk through puddles. Children are not afraid to hope for the best possible outcome!

What happened to relegate hope to an afterthought? We try to maneuver through the struggles of life and say, "I'm fine. I don't need hope. I can make it without it."

When God is saying, "Excuse Me, I've given you everything you need."

Everything you need to survive isn't found while attending Harvard Business School. Everything you need to thrive doesn't come from the counselor's couch or from streaming your favorite show. It's already in you.

Because we've refused to make a choice and because we've lived serendipitously, we have a casual relationship even with ourselves, and hope remains dormant. But hope still resides. I dare you to give yourself permission to live. Dine occasionally rather than just eating. Skip rather than walk. Sing in the rain and walk through puddles. What do you have to lose? Hope.

What are you choosing to do today to wake up the hope inside you?

I have some dear friends, a married couple, who enjoy going to the golf course together. He plays golf; she takes off her shoes and strolls in the pristine grass.

Well, Rick, how is walking on a golf course barefoot going to give me hope?

I would suggest that you're asking the wrong question. The better question is:

How does walking barefoot through the grass affect me in a positive manner?

The simplest activity—activities children participate in without planning or scheduling—has potential to put you in a better frame of mind. At some level, the activity likely releases endorphins and increases the serotonin level in your brain. The exercise introduces more oxygen into the blood stream. Why is it we shy away from taking our shoes off when walking on the grass? Because we have perceived expectations. And guess what perceived expectations do … they keep hope locked up.

Hope is active, dynamic, thrilling, and energetic. We might say we hope, but we aren't matching our words with our actions.

"This situation will work out for good, Bob."

"I sure hope so," mumbled Bob, shaking his head.

That's not hope.

With hope, it's possible to be in jail and be free. With hope, it is possible to enter a high school cafeteria and have a dining experience. With hope, it's possible to take a frequent flight of fancy from the human to the humane. I'm talking about a spirit energized. I'm talking about a different way of looking at life.

What brings you hope? "That we won't have World War III."

No.

"Well, what brings me hope is that my bills will be paid off and then I can...."

Sorry to interrupt. But, no.

"That I make a choice to live a better quality of life."

Getting warmer.

"Taking my shoes off and walking on the grass. And tapping into the God-given hope inside me to transform my attitude and expectation about the future!"

Bingo.

At the movies

I love watching Hallmark movies—especially the Christmas selections. But before you judge me, here's why. Hallmark movies are sappy, predictable, and follow the most basic *film noir* formula of inevitably discovering your soulmate and falling in love ... and I'm hooked—a huge fan!

Each movie begins with a problem to solve that usually takes our wandering hero to some lovely and pristine location amidst snow-covered landscapes and the soft glow of the Christmas lights. And despite the plot's twists and turns, our hero dramatically discovers new meaning and love in between commercial breaks. Like a Norman Rockwell painting, life is portrayed in beautifully symmetrical hues. Every time.

And in the end, I cry. Every time.

You can't apply this to all movies, that's for sure. But can we apply this kind of innocent hope to life? I believe we can.

After years of confusion and complication, I find hope in the clear and the simple. After a season of unevenness and inconsistency, I find hope in stability and the predictable. Your variables may differ from mine, but the principle remains the same: Discovering hope is a practical activity, often located during the regular routine days of life. What Hallmark movies reinforce to me is that humans were never designed to find hope externally. Hope resides within each of us and becomes activated in our lives through the choices we make. And those choices can be as simple as choosing less confusion by ordering your thoughts. Or, choosing to give yourself permission to include in your day one thought of gratitude among the stable of negative thoughts.

Hope at work

Hope is staggeringly practical. Even in your career.

Do you want to get beyond your everyday shallow circumstances you try to hide behind? For example, "Life would be better if my boss wasn't such a jerk."

Most people create a list of circumstances they allow to determine their happiness, health, and peace. But you're in charge by simply reassessing the situation. Often, the first step is to eliminate the false trappings you hide behind so you can justify your desire not to grow. Once again, "feelings" are dictating behaviors.

"How can I make it through downsizing? Every single quarter we're getting new employees and they're younger and more talented. I'm freaking out!"

After years of being on university faculties, and at Texas A&M a member of the football staff, I experienced similar thoughts. Every year, for example, the faculty department head or, in football, the head coach would hire new people and my first thought was, *What if they're better than me?* Suddenly, my existence was threatened.

At some point, you realize that to get better you have to make better choices. Like choosing a mind-set that new hires should motivate you to be even better for the greater good of the organization. In other words, I choose hope. Let's be clear, we all must deal with emotions and thoughts that naturally arise, but we can choose hope. When you choose hope rather than being motivated by emotion, you realize the possibilities, like learning something new from others, or rising to and above perceived challenges. Such a shift moves us one step away from ourselves. Now, we begin to consider the possibility that maybe a new hire can help us reach our goals and achieve our objectives—whether it's building the strongest communication faculty in the nation, or winning a national championship. Note: The mind-set change began with a simple and pragmatic choice to hope for a better outcome.

By adjusting my attitude, by making a demand on my heart and mind, I found hope.

Controlling the pain

Some people have love affairs with sex, some addicted to drugs, others to alcohol, some with spending, and some with creating false identities. Humans are going to find *something* or *someone* to help medicate the pain.

In the midst of my grief, I decided that God could not medicate my pain. It wasn't that I did not love God; it was because I lost my trust in Him. I was angry at Him. I would never sleep with somebody else's wife, but I could use feelings to protect and soothe my pain. I did not do illegal drugs, but I became a food addict. Gluttony was an "acceptable" sin, and it soothed my pain. And it was something I could control.

It might be a father who left you. It might be a wife who left you. It might be a boss who played bait and switch on you. It might be the abuse in your past or the fact that you got burned badly by someone. But for whatever reason, you may have trust issues—mixed with seething anger. *It's me against the world and I'm only going to allow things close to me that I can control. I'm never going to get hurt again.*

I can remember being on airplanes and saying to myself, "I am going to eat anything I want when I land and nobody is going to tell me otherwise." I believe some of this desire for control also came from oncologists telling me for years, "You can't go on vacation. You can't do this. You need to cancel that."

But I discovered hope was something I could control. The valley is the incubator for hope. Because without the valley experience, we're not desperate enough to *want* to change.

So, let's be clear. I'm *not* asking you to change. I'm asking if you *want to* change.

Exercising hope

There's nothing to earn. There aren't seven steps to follow. Hope is in you.

Before you finish this chapter, you can choose to unlock hope in your life.

Hope is a quality of every human spirit that places
a transformative demand upon our heart to believe
for the absolute best outcome.

What's one area that's worrying you, or hurting your heart right now?

Is it possible, even though the situation may be challenging, one small bit of good could come from the pain? Despite what our feelings scream, despite the bitter reality, we know the answer is *yes*.

Now, imagine. Dig deep and refuse to come up empty.

What is one possible good outcome?

Pause and reflect on the question above. Don't be afraid to hope.

Chapter 6

AFRAID TO HOPE

Hope is a quality of every human spirit that places
a transformative demand upon our heart to believe
for the absolute best outcome.

Despite my definition of hope, why was I not hoping?

So, here's the problem. If the capacity to hope is within us all, something was blocking the expansion of my capacity. I wanted to hope. I desired to hope. But something was preventing me from taking that step from hopeless to hopeful.

I now have the perspective of two decades to reflect upon the "whys" that I could not figure out while in the valley of despair.

Here's the best news. If you are willing to embrace the essence of this one central thought, maybe it will take less time for you to make the move over to choose hope:

I was terrified over the possibility of living again. I was frightened about the prospect of "feeling" again. I was fearful to fully live. To completely give. To totally trust. I became afraid to hope.

Desperation, discouragement, and loneliness can produce such a depressed state that one's thinking becomes irrational. In the midst of a whirlwind of emotion, my thinking was not motivated by logic—biblical or otherwise. I was consumed by how I felt. I hoped once, and everything worked out fantastic. Dream job. Dream wife. Dream children. Dream life. Suddenly, the valley produced trust issues. I was afraid to trust. Afraid to live. Afraid to dream. Afraid to read the Bible. Afraid to trust God.

I became afraid to hope.

A favorite passage in Scripture always has been Proverbs 3:5-6, which states, "Trust in the Lord with all your heart, and do not lean on your own understanding. In all your ways acknowledge Him, and He will make your paths straight" (NASB).

In the valley, I chose to reinterpret that scripture to fit my state of mind:

Trust in nothing that might have the possibility to break your heart and make you hurt again. You shall depend on your understanding of things. Acknowledge your feelings—and choose the path of least pain and heartache.

I was afraid to hope. And that fear caused me to stop living.

My feelings became my security blanket. I used my feelings to justify a protection from hurt at all cost. My feelings granted me permission to do what I pleased, and to numb that which was not pleasing. What I did not realize was the devastating minefield these choices were creating in my heart and manifesting in my life. Before long, I was living a shallow, superficial life—which was purposefully out of touch and physically out of control.

It became more manageable to be fearful than faithful. Being fearful meant my feelings could control and determine and justify and protect. Being faithful would mean loss of control, no justifications, and an unprotected heart.

It was at this point in my journey, right in the midst of this internal conflict, exactly at the point when I could have gone either way—the way of hope or hopeless—that something amazingly shocking occurred that forced me to confront my fears. It would become the turning point of my life.

Daring to hope

Most of us deal with anger issues at one time or another. Yet, none of us are ever really taught how to manage those feelings. As a result, we advance into our careers and family lives not realizing that our hearts are not well, and thus the chance for experiencing authentic hope is minimized.

Even though I was hurting and avoiding, my sons and I were progressing fairly well. Even with this gaping hole in our hearts we figured out a way to recreate normalcy. I'll always be grateful for the families who offered my boys a break with weekend visits. As for me, I finally figured my friends were right … it was time for me to move on.

Just one problem. How?

Life changed for me the very moment I saw her in the audience. By now, I was speaking again, this particular morning at a prayer breakfast engagement in our community. When I saw her, well, I can't explain the sensation, a feeling I'd only experienced once before. I immediately lost my place in my notes, as my mouth became as dry as a parched bench on a hot Texas day. After a few awkward moments, I regained my composure, rambled through my notes, concluded my talk, greeted some guests, and most importantly, asked someone "Who's that woman?!"

There were a few other women over the previous months who had expressed "interest." With no emotional attachment, I dismissed advances as nothing more than those who felt sorry for a widower.

When your wife dies, your friends—with good intentions, though misguided—attempt to introduce you to "that girl"! The women were all very nice and attractive. It wasn't them, it was me. I was scared. But on this particular early morning, this woman was very different than any other. And my heart knew it the moment our eyes met.

Her name was Janet Butcher, a local schoolteacher who moved to Texas from Ohio. She was, and is, breathtakingly beautiful. And she was single. (*Did I just hear angels sing?*) When I met her after the event, I was stunned by how beautiful she was, and discouraged by her complete lack of interest in me!

It's something we laugh about today. You see, back then I had no idea she and her best friends had prayed for me and the boys since the day of Trina's funeral. I had no idea God had selected this woman to be my future soulmate. All I knew was she was hot and I wanted to meet her. When I approached her, she was a bit standoffish. Janet would later explain that it's one thing to pray about meeting someone, and a completely different feeling when you're actually face-to-face.

After some mutual friends arranged an awkward "group date," I summoned the courage to call Janet directly and ask for a formal lunch date at a local restaurant. My son Jeremiah said I tried on no less than ten outfits. All I remember is sitting across the table from Janet, and being so mesmerized I could not eat. That was a first!

My excitement was tempered with another new feeling. As a widower, dating was just plain weird. On one hand, your heart is exploding with excitement. Simultaneously, you feel guilt for "cheating" on your wife, while hearing whispers from others and seeing looks of skepticism on their faces. Weird.

Before going any further, let me state most people celebrated my courtship with Janet. A few didn't and resented me for moving on. One "friend" even warned that my boys might *forget their mom* if I remarried.

Over the years, I've had the opportunity to help widows, widowers, and their families navigate through the awkward minefield of new romance. I tell them, "It's your life! Live it—without feeling pressure from the expectations of others."

Often, a widower will ask, "When will I know if I am ready to date?" Great question. Everyone is different, and there may be several missteps before you take a step. Then again, maybe not. My simple response is, "You will know." French philosopher Blasé Pascal captured the essence of my belief when he stated, *"The heart knows what the heart knows."* Not everyone will understand or celebrate. Just remember, you're not living to satisfy the expectations of people. One beautiful benefit from living in the valley is developing the mind-set that you no longer live according to others. My primary concern was for my sons and Trina's brother Benjamin.

For the most part, family and friends were thrilled I'd found love, and that my boys would be cared for by a mom. Trina's final wish was that her children not go through life without a mama. She also told me, "Honey, you need a wife. You weren't meant to be alone." Selfless to the end.

As crazy as it may sound, I believe Trina worked with God to pick Janet. Janet is beautiful, talented, intelligent, and very compassionate. Among Janet's greatest qualities, an undaunting graciousness she inherited from her mother. It was Janet who insisted that pictures of Trina remain on the walls as long as needed. It was Janet who reached out to Trina's family.

Today, we're as close to Trina's brother and his family as ever. And, it was Janet who insisted on adopting our boys, Jeremiah and Andrew, as her own. In our family, we choose not to use the term "step" to refer to children or mom. Our boys grew up honored to have two mothers: *Mom Trina*, their biological mom, and *Mom Janet*, their adopted mom. Were there awkward moments? Absolutely. Were there uncomfortable times of adjustment? Certainly. But we were all honest with our feelings as we embraced our blended family.

One funny moment that brings us unrelenting joy is when we reflect what our youngest Andrew once said when Mom Janet pressed him to share what was really in his heart. After a few moments of contemplation, Andrew said, "My greatest concern is … I just don't know if I'm ready for another woman to tell me what to do!"

I believe there will be a special place in heaven for those who marry widows and widowers. For they must have a maturity, a self-confidence, and a grace that very few possess.

Faith and hope

Our courtship was from the pages of a fairytale. Janet had never been married and waited until she was into her mid-thirties. I never imagined my heart would find love again, and had to pinch myself each day of our courtship. I proposed to Janet three months after I met her, and we were married within a year. And in terms of those fears, let's just say the excitement of the moment meant I didn't have to deal with them.

But for the time being, we were enjoying the bliss of romance. Our mutual families were thrilled, our friends were excited, and we were on top of the world. Many of the same family members and friends, who had grieved with us a few years earlier, were back at that College Station church to witness the miracle of matrimony.

Nearly a year to the day we were married, our third child—Zachary Benton Rigsby was born—on my birthday! Zachary's birth affected me greatly and represented physical manifestation of hope restored. Zachary's birth reaffirmed my faith in God and caused my heart to once again believe that all things are possible.

If Zachary's birth was beyond my wildest expectation, eighteen months later Janet gave birth to our fourth son, Joshua Wellington Rigsby, or "Pup" as he is known because he's the pup of the litter. Pup was hope personified. He looks like me, acts like me, laughs like me. He's the "me" before the valley and I love all he represents.

By the time their younger brothers were born, Jeremiah and Andrew were teenagers, so sibling rivalry—for the most part—was not an issue. Rather, it was a love fest every day, as the house bustled with energy, joy, and laughter that can only come from toddlers running wild. What a difference a few years had made.

In retrospect, I mustered just enough faith to get me through the valley. But if you asked me if I had hope, the answer is no. In retrospect, hope was always there. I just could not locate it. A glaring example is contained in the first paragraph of this section on *Faith and Hope*. Read again how I began sentence number three in this section's first paragraph:

I never imagined my heart would find love again.

I never imagined. Did I have faith? I think so. Hope? Absolutely not. The fact is, I had neither.

So, what's the difference between faith and hope?

Most people can probably give a pretty good definition of faith, but draw a blank on hope. In my experience, faith has always been elevated above hope in terms of teaching and practice.

You may be familiar with the scriptural passage that states: "Now faith is the substance of things hoped for, the evidence of things not seen" (Hebrews 11:1 NKJV). A reexamination of this verse has broadened my thinking about the role and function of hope in our lives.

If faith is the *substance* of that which is hoped for, hope becomes the prerequisite for faith. In other words, it's impossible to have faith unless first you have hope. Unless you can hope for a better outcome than your present reality, faith won't be a reality for you. This verse is used to teach what faith is, but I've never heard it used to help us understand what hope is, and how hope is connected to faith.

Faith can only be built on a hope-filled heart. Show me a person who has no faith and I'll show you a person who has no hope.

For so many years, I wondered why my faith wavered, until I realized I was lacking the foundation: hope. In the valley, I was too busy feeling sorry for myself to hope. I never considered hoping that I would remarry or hoping that I would have more children, or hoping that there would be some sense of normalcy to replace the nightmare we were living. Rather than hoping, I spent my time and energy lamenting, which made me question my faith. And by now, you're beginning to realize there's a war on hope.

Control and trust

If you've ever talked to people who've suffered abuse, many will tell you they live a life of secrecy and protect themselves by controlling their environment. Have you ever felt that way?

I only trusted what I could manipulate, and even had a motto: *In me I trust.*

I trust me because, God, You let me down. As a matter of fact, I'm mad at You for allowing this to happen! How can You expect me to trust You? I treated God as though He was a celestial vending machine. I put my coin in, pulled the lever, and got the intended result. Until I didn't.

Here's the bare truth. For the first half of my life, things went so well that there was no need for a foundation of hope. That is an arrogant statement, born out of ignorance. I lived a charmed life, accomplished all my dreams with little resistance. So, when I hit rock bottom, one of the first things I discovered was I had spent a life practicing situational faith, and never developed the disciplines required to build a solid foundation of hope. Simply stated, I was a Christian a long time before I was a seriously committed Christian.

When you live a trouble-free life, it's hard to see a need to *hope for* the best possible outcome. All of a sudden, "trouble-free" no longer describes my existence. I am in the valley with no roadmap how to escape. My faith was taking blows and I was reeling. I had no explanations and no answers. When I couldn't find answers, I began to blame everything and everybody, especially God.

I'm going to medicate my pain so I don't have to think about You or the situation. I'll show You, God! You think You're sovereign, but I'll control what I want to control.

I made a choice not to live a critical element of life. During the good times, I should have been practicing hope, preparing to hope, looking for the best possible outcomes. Instead, I suddenly found myself in a valley with no compass. This was not the *American Dream* I was used to living. One thing was certain. If I was going to survive the nightmare, I could not be concerned with building some type of foundation of hope. I had to stop hurting. I had to medicate my pain.

In the history of the United States, the "American Dream" is a construct based on the protestant work ethic. I taught this concept in classes which focused on media and popular culture at Texas A&M University. The construct is built in this fashion:

A. *If I go to the right school and receive a good education;*

B. *If I can land the right job;*

C. *If I marry the right person;*

D. *Then my life will be a fairytale filled with riches and success.*

The problem is A + B + C never equals D.

In reality, it's the failures of life—the knockdowns, the setbacks, the adversities, the valleys—that produce the potential to grow successfully. When you've depleted all resources and see no way of escape, you're forced to make a choice. You can choose to figure out a better way or just coast—what I call *going through the motions*. I chose the latter and ignored a dormant opportunity: *You have a free will. You don't have to self-destruct. You can make better choices.*

I avoided pain at all costs and in the process, avoided the truth. The avoidance of truth comes with a price, but I didn't care. Painless is the heart not required to face reality, or so I thought. The pursuit of pleasure is an alluring drug that masks the harshness of reality. This was my life. Nothing entered my heart that would cause me any pain. *God would never hurt me again,* I resolved.

I even protected myself from certain "triggers" that might cause me to feel pain. In fact, to this day, some two decades later, I have difficulty watching movies that involve someone dying. I would much rather see comedies with "happily ever after" endings even if it means predictable plots and overused storylines. I want to see the "American Dream" personified without failures, setbacks, or pain.

How's that for living an alternative reality?

My cluttered closet

I survived the valley, or so I thought. Didn't need that foundation of hope after all. Finally, life was good again. At least that's what I wanted you to believe. I married Janet, the new love of my life. Jeremiah and Andrew seemed much happier and were laughing and enjoying life again. And the additions of Zachary and Joshua made for high energy, constant unpredictability, and fun-filled adventures. Once again, life was as it should be. Or was it?

Falling in love with Janet had given me a new lease on life and a justification to go, do, spend, buy, and above all, eat. My eating began growing out of control during Trina's illness, and passing, and those poor habits continued into my new marriage to Janet. Throughout those years, I hovered around 400 pounds. To accommodate my public life of speaking, I purchased tailored suits and handmade shirts. Brioni, Zegna, and Stefano Ricci had become dear friends.

My closet also held one hundred pairs of shoes from brands like Ferragamo, Bruno Magli, Prada, and Church's of England, in addition to topcoats, leather coats, evening coats, and every accessory imaginable. If I wanted it, I bought it. Why not? Eating made me happy. Buying made me happy. And happiness is the goal of life, right?

Here's the problem. Although I was happily married and enjoying life with our four sons, I had never dealt with the deep pain of having no hope. I covered my compulsions with expensive clothes, but—as we say in Texas—I was a *hot mess*.

Act I

Sooner or later, "fear," that primary enemy of hope, will manifest itself. And, it wasn't just manifesting in my weight and wardrobe, but in my relationships. After a few years of bliss, something began changing in our marriage.

Janet began to notice that I would lose my temper over the slightest thing. Our older boys—especially Jeremiah, noticed an angry "edge" to every conversation. I recall once, Jeremiah said, "Dad, I just need you to talk with me and not always lecture me." But I was not cluing in. If you know me, you know I'm typically the happiest camper in town. However, more and more, my family, especially Janet, lovingly brought the temper outbursts to my attention.

I remember her words exactly. "Honey, this is not you. What's going on? This is not your personality. It's not normal for you to get upset so easily."

I'd been exposed—not just with Janet, but to myself. I knew that I had been medicating my pain and could justify it because I wasn't hurting anyone. But now circumstances had changed. My sweetheart, and even on occasion my boys, told me something was wrong. It began affecting the atmosphere at home.

These conversations—primarily between Janet and me—initiated the most uncomfortable time periods in my life. The most *devastating* time period was immediately after Trina's death. The most *uncomfortable* time period was the delayed aftermath of unresolved issues relating to her death. Janet was forcing me to go deeper, some place I had never been and certainly did not want to visit.

So, for a season in my life, I went into my office every single morning, alone. I closed the door, closed the blinds, and dimmed the lights. I didn't turn on any music or TV, nor did I open the Bible. I'd just sit and demand that God tell me what was going on. I repeated this cycle every single day, whether at home or on the road. This season lasted a few years, yet it seemed like an eternity.

I wasn't ready for what happened.

I wish I could tell you I was super-spiritual and heard from God right away. The truth is, the first few days, I fell asleep. I discovered that during my "quiet time," I was imagining everything from which restaurant I'd visit that night in Chicago, to calculating whether I could squeeze in a trip to Neiman's shoe section before heading to the airport.

After a few weeks of showing up faithfully, I began to sense something in my heart. It wasn't an audible voice, but more like an impression that pounded inside my chest. I began to realize I was mad at God! I was angry at Him for ignoring my prayers despite my years of service to Him. I preached all over the world. Didn't that count for anything? I was mad at God for taking Trina from us. How could a loving God do this, especially a woman who was so wonderful?

I remember screaming one morning, "What kind of God are You to take a mother away from her babies?" And, to my surprise, I realized my anger extended beyond God. I was mad at Trina for abandoning us.

If you haven't lost a spouse, you likely will not understand the anger aimed at my dead wife. The reality was Trina fought harder to stay alive than anyone I'd ever witnessed. Logically I knew this. But rarely do grieving people exist in a logical reality. I was mad at Trina. She left us. She left me. She left her boys. I was seething with anger.

Reflecting on this period in my life reminded me of something Janet once mentioned. She believes 99 percent of people have some source of hidden anger in their lives. We become masters of deception and camouflage the anger with well-manicured facades, something I know all too well. Janet added, "Very few of us are taught how to deal with disappointments or grief at a young age, so we grow up with unresolved issues inside, that at some point, will manifest themselves in relationships."

I began the slow process of facing my anger. To my shock, I discovered I was "open" to discussing some lifestyle changes that would promote better mental, physical, and spiritual health. Little steps had to be taken.

And the first step was shifting from avoidance to acknowledgement.

I wish I could tell you my cravings and temper vanished overnight. It took months. Years. But it began with the small step of making a choice. I made a choice to stay at it. Along the way, a miracle took place. After years of long talks and one-sided arguments, I made peace with God. I also had many long talks and one-sided shouting matches with Trina. After some time, I concluded she never meant or desired to leave or abandon us. And while I still ache on occasion, and although a tear is never too far from my eyes, I can honestly say, *It is well with my soul.*

Act II

After a few years, I had corralled my temper, and established a healthier lifestyle. Slowly, I began confronting my anger, and started discovering how making different choices could produce different outcomes. Despite my objections, God wanted to go much deeper than I was comfortable with.

I've often said, it's a lot easier to mow over a root than to actually pull it out of the ground. This surgery was going to be painful, and there would be no anesthesia. The experience left an indelible lesson: change demands discomfort. Do not expect significant change if you're not significantly uncomfortable.

I remember the moment as if it were today. I was standing in front of my closet—a closet packed with stuff that suddenly was too big for me to wear. As I boxed up the suits, shirts, and shoes—some items never opened—I heard God's voice in such a way it scared me!

"Could all this clutter in your closet be an indication of your heart— a heart with so much clutter there's no room for Me?"

It hit me like a ton of bricks. Years of being motivated by feelings and medicating symptoms had cluttered my heart with resentment, pain, rejection, anger, and most of all fear. Being afraid to hope had come with a hefty price. My choice to self-medicate had packed on pounds, loaded my heart with destructive emotional time bombs, and filled my life with unnecessary junk. And now, my choices to avoid and medicate issues were converging with a force that threatened the peace and joy of my closest relationships.

Can you relate? Right now, I ask you to pause and examine *your* closet. And I'm not talking about the one in your bedroom. Making a choice to self-medicate produces robust enemies of hope, such as:

1. A lack of trust

2. A lack of faith

3. Dwelling on circumstances

4. Anger

5. Fear

6. Regret

7. A self-centered attitude

What I didn't understand then is crystal clear now. I chose those behaviors because no matter where I looked, I couldn't find hope. Real hope. Hope that's alive, energetic, and transformative. More accurately, I chose those behaviors because I could not imagine a better life. I could not envision better outcomes. I was afraid to hope.

I lived in a world of empty words and catch phrases. My world offered an appearance that said, "I'm fine." My world was well manicured. I was a college professor, character coach, and chaplain for a football team, minister, and motivational speaker. On the outside, everything "appeared" well-manicured. Everything was orderly and outlined on the outside, but on the inside, my closet was cluttered. Then, with one question, Janet challenged me to open the closet door by asking, "Honey, what's going on with you?" I was exposed. Before long, the enemies of hope would be exposed also.

I will discuss these enemies of hope later in the book. However, I mention them here to get you thinking about potential enemies lurking in your closet.

As I uncluttered my closet (my heart), I began to unpack hidden hurts, while loosening the reigns of control. I allowed myself to trust other people, and receive their love and wisdom. My eyes became open to examples of people saddled with the baggage of cluttered closets. For example, I realized Moses in the Bible had a closet cluttered with arrogance, ego, and self-righteousness, and it kept him in the wilderness for forty years. I made a vow that I wouldn't stay in the valley and miss my promised land. And I started looking at my suffering differently. My suffering opened my eyes to my destiny. It's hard to say that the worst thing that could've ever happened to me was the best thing, but I just said it.

But Trina knew the secret way before I did. "It's not how *long* I live, but it's *how* I live."

I couldn't receive more hope and healing until I made more room.

Open the door

Is your soul so cluttered there's no room for hope?

If your heart is cluttered, it's probably a sign of your priorities. And it shows that hope isn't a priority. I'm not telling you this to condemn you. As you know from my story, few of us even knew the true definition of hope.

Hope is a lifestyle. Remember our working definition:

> *Hope is a quality of every human spirit that places*
> *a transformative demand upon our heart to believe*
> *for the absolute best outcome.*

Hope is dynamic, it's a moving force, a quality of life. Hope changes you and equips you to change your perspective and perhaps your world.

If you have a cluttered closet, there's no room for hope. Open the door to your heart and take a good look at what you see. For me, I had to acknowledge I was in hot pursuit of that which was shallow and frivolous to medicate my pain. I said enough is enough.

I made a mess of my life. But I had some iron-clad excuses. Why have you made a mess of your life? Are you now ready to admit some things to yourself? Are you ready to make some changes? If you say yes, now we can start growing your capacity for hope.

If you say no, I can't do anything about it. Thanks for reading this far, I wish you well. I hope you come back and visit sometime soon.

The issue is a reluctance to overcome fear in order to grow. The priorities we establish to numb the pain are actually designed for our demise.

The valley is actually designed to declutter, to strip off everything that holds us back. Want to pull a wagon loaded with stuff throughout your life? You do have a choice. Open the closet door and face your fear. You really don't have to wait for a spouse to ask you. And once you make this critical choice, you are one step away from discovering hope!

Chapter 7

EXISTING

I encounter many people who, for lack of a better explanation, are merely existing. Some are in valleys, but others seem to be succeeding in businesses, boardrooms, and classrooms.

Here's what those who are "existing" have in common: hopelessness. Can you relate?

Something has occurred in your life which has disappointed you. When you are disappointed, you lose perspective and seek to remedy the situation, rather than seeking how to benefit from it. You know well that my remedies, including indulgences of various types, resulted in a cluttered closet and relational challenges. I found it much easier to exist without hope rather than dream of a better possible outcome.

Right now, right in the midst of your disappointment, ask yourself a simple question: Does my disappointment contain any benefit or opportunity? I know that is probably the last question you want to ask. But consider the old adage, *every cloud has a silver lining*. My wise father used to say, "Son, there's a bright side somewhere." Henry David Thoreau put it like this: "If we are quiet enough and ready, we shall find compensation in every disappointment." I was not quiet enough in the valley, nor was I ready. As a result, I existed there for far too long. But you don't have to!

You may find this hard to believe, but disappointment can be beneficial in the short term because it encourages evaluation and contemplation. In other words, disappointment is a *silver* opportunity to face reality, evaluate the situation to determine what is and is not effective, and learn what was right or wrong about your response.

I wish I would have asked myself three simple questions when saddled with the weight of disappointment. "Am I expecting a better outcome?" "Is there something stopping me from expecting a better outcome?" "What step must I take to begin living a better outcome?"

Do you think these questions can help you get over being afraid to hope? Give it a shot. What do you have to lose?

Looking back two decades, I clearly see what I refused to acknowledge then.

The opportunity in my disappointment was to stand, to continue living, to not give up.

If you get nothing else from this book get this: If you're afraid to hope, you will never see the opportunity. All you will see is the disappointment.

I was disappointed for so long that I began to get discouraged. Even after I came out of my original valley, I continued to struggle well into a new marriage. In fact, to this day I struggle with discouragement. When you're discouraged, you have lost your courage and your enthusiasm.

Whenever my father—the wisest man I ever met, though a third-grade dropout—was discouraged, he would go beyond himself and try to meet a need. Try this: in the midst of discouragement, ask yourself, is there a need or a purpose that you can accomplish—something that will force you to take baby steps away from your feelings into a healthier, more productive life.

If you are afraid to hope, you will never see the opportunity to meet a need or connect to a purpose. Life becomes all about you, and believe me, all you will see and sense is discouragement.

Janet's challenge to find the source of my outbursts forced me to go deeper than I ever imagined. I began to realize that hope was always there, right in the same place as trouble. But giving in to the pain of being uncomfortable or the fear of being exposed, it was much more convenient to exist in disappointment.

Justify and blame

For whatever reason, a natural compulsion of human beings is to justify behavior and assign blame. It's a lot easier to live this way. The temporal delusion of feeling unscathed is a beautiful alternative to face a harsh reality.

I'm no exception, despite great training from my parents. My father used to tell me, "Son, when I was a kid, growing up in rural Texas as an African-American, I had to get off the sidewalk to allow men of another color to walk on the sidewalk."

"Dad, you're kidding. Did you fight or what?"

"Son, there's a word for that; it's called 'history.' We live in the present."

Suffice to say, my brother and I weren't allowed to make excuses regarding our color, our neighborhood, or our family's income level. We weren't allowed to justify bad choices. And generally, I made good choices and enjoyed positive results.

Everything changed when I found myself in the valley. I could justify existing because it required very little effort. I became proficient in the language of justification. Surely my intense pain deserved the food or impulse I prescribed. I defended my case on a daily basis as if I was in front of a judge in a court of law. I presumed that I needed to justify my behaviors to God, the ultimate Judge. As such, I recall uttering such lines as:

This is the reason why I'm angry and frustrated. This is the reason why I don't trust You. This is the reason why I overeat. This is the reason I am motivated by how I feel. This is the reason why I travel so much. This is the reason why I'm easily distracted.

And my powerful closing argument:

And if You don't like it, You shouldn't have put me in that situation to begin with. Who are You to tell me that I ought to change my ways based on the situation that You put me in?

Mine was an unrighteous indignation. But it appeased every sensibility I had at the time. My goal was to preserve what little I had left. The problem was, I didn't have anything left. Afraid of what I would discover if I made any attempt to move on, I was completely motivated by my feelings. And my feelings were under attack. When your feelings and sensibilities are threatened, you fight back.

It's a natural visceral reaction, but a destructive lifestyle.

The language of justification

I developed a language in the valley—a language of justification. After all, this was the fight of my life and how dare You tell me how I should live?

At the time, I only had two responsibilities—one was named Jeremiah and one was named Andrew, my two children. Everything else was negotiable and optional.

There's a communication theory called *Uses and Gratification.* An example of this is how we're gratified by the way in which we use a particular stimuli. My studies focused on media criticism, and thus I was interested in how people used television programming and the gratifications associated with that usage. For example, it's interesting to observe a toddler who's focused on a toy, until a favorite television commercial captures his attention. That toddler, according to this theory, isn't so much gratified by the advertisement but the familiarity he has with the ad. Being able to recall something familiar gratifies us. It's the same sensation adults have when we get the occasional *Jeopardy* question correct. (Or maybe that's just me.)

Justifying my behavior pacified me. The problem with this kind of attitude is, number one, the slightest breeze can knock you right back to the lowest point of the valley. Number two, you're off balance physically, mentally, financially, emotionally, or spiritually, and you cannot perform well at anything.

You're like a person responsible for spinning twelve plates at the same time. Problem is, you don't really care if they fall or not. You've checked out of life.

But the greatest issue, with being stuck defending my case, is I lived in denial.

The root of bitterness

My brother-in-law David Butcher is a man's man, a real outdoorsman. I asked him once, "How long does it take to cut down a tree?"

"Could be as little as ten minutes, even for a pretty large tree," he answered.

Then I asked, "After you've cut it down, how long does it take to remove the roots?"

He paused a moment, then replied, "You know, depending on the number of people helping, it could take a full day or even a couple of days."

Therein lies the problem. Why sweat life when you can merely exist? Why go through all the time and energy to pull a root when you can cover the stump with branches in seconds? Not only does it seem less painful this way, but your yard (your life) is spared the pain and scars of major surgery.

Here's where the language of justification kicks into high gear. With no visible evidence of the hell raging in my heart, when people asked how I was doing I could say, "Just fine." I would repeat that lie numerous times daily for months. Years.

That's the language of defending your case and not dealing with reality. I was searching for something I would never find—ever—normalcy in the past.

Please hear me. It wasn't for lack of trying. If you're dealing with pain, I know you're trying. And if you want to be an agent of hope to someone you care about, know they're trying—whether it looks like *your* kind of trying or not.

Decades later, with mega doses of hope, I see clearly. The first thing I should have done is pause and acknowledge I was making bad choices with devastating repercussions.

I can't go back. Neither can you. But if you're in the middle of a disappointing and discouraging situation, and medicating the pain with anything but hope, will you pause with me? Will you take a breath and say out loud, *I'm making some bad choices right now. These choices are only digging me deeper into the valley.*

Isolation in the valley

I turned down so many wonderful invitations in the valley. It was purposeful isolation.

"Why don't you come over for dinner?"

I graciously declined, and ungraciously thought, *I don't want to be a fifth wheel. I don't want to be the object of your sorrow.* (See how my mind worked? Wonderful people were simply inviting me to dinner and I concocted a twisted agenda and painful experience.)

It *s*eemed like everywhere I went people were enjoying life and having a good time. Then, I'd show up, and suddenly the mood changed dramatically. I grew tired of being the cause of sadness and despair.

To be fair, and despite my dark delusions, I was 1 percent justified in my feelings about social gatherings, 1 percent of the time. Let me set the scene for you. Imagine you're me for a minute. (A frightening scenario, I know.) You've mustered all your courage and gathered just enough hope to drive to the dinner party.

As you park, you think to yourself, *Hey, this isn't so bad. This might be just what I need.*

As you walk through the door friends are chatting and laughing. *Wow, I haven't been in such a positive environment in months.*

As you approach two friends in the living room, their eyes meet yours, and their faces instantly change from smiling to somber, from carefree to concerned. Their voices change to a whisper.

"Hi, Rick. How ... are you doing?"

And for you, the lights dim and the party turns into a funeral. All over again.

You don't even like sympathy cards, so why in the world would you want to walk into a real-life one?

Okay, you can stop being me now. (You're welcome.)

When you're deep in the valley it's an easy choice between (what feels like) an awkward social event and going to the Golden Corral on endless-shrimp night.

Pain, shame, and isolation create a downward spiral. Purposeful isolation is a destructive choice.

Kenneth Stampp, one of the most prolific historians of the 20th century, helped to advance our understanding of America's Civil War years and among other topics the peculiar institution of slavery. Stampp noted that the Master's mentality when encountering revolting slaves was demonically simple: If you could isolate the slave, you could kill his spirit.

Doesn't that bring the danger of isolation to light?

Yet, many of us would rather exist in isolation rather than search for hope.

As a minister, I have heard so many people say, "Pastor Rick, I don't have to attend church to serve God!" And while that statement is correct, what they do not understand is that human beings need community for survival. And the worst thing we can do in a time of trouble is to isolate. Nothing, absolutely nothing produces hopelessness like struggling with your best friends, Misery and Rejection.

Purposeful isolation is the worst choice you can make. We can't flip a switch and stop the pain. We can't take an eraser and wipe out the growing shame. But we can do something about isolation, today.

After acknowledging you're in the fight of your life, and how some of your choices are devastatingly destructive, ask yourself, *is isolation the best choice for my future?*

Isolation is dangerous because it's based on a counterfeit hope—the belief that encounters with other people will automatically reinforce negative feelings. But here's where real hope shines, if you'll just open the door a bit.

Isolating hope

Instead of using your creative capacity to imagine the worst, make a demand on your spirit to believe for the best possible outcome.

What if God is up to something out there in the wide world? Maybe I should take some steps out of the valley, because maybe—just maybe—God is out there and He's already orchestrated something good for me.

What if—right in the midst of disappointment—you challenged yourself to look for an opportunity and the silver lining?

I literally got to a point where I could no longer just exist. Something had to change. For me, it was sparked by my wife asking what was wrong with me. What will be your catalyst for change? Or, will you continue to be afraid to hope?

I would encourage you to cease defending yourself with the language of justification. Plead guilty as a first step toward settling the case and eventually receiving mercy.

Remain stuck, or take a step.

What if?

When you're in the valley, you don't see the great potential to develop wisdom. You don't see the great possibilities. You certainly don't see the opportunities. You see nothing but the struggle.

Please hear me. The valley is loaded with wisdom. If you dare to think about it, many of your best days have come on the heels of your worst disappointments. Why is that? Because a valley experience offers the opportunity to reinvent, to stretch, to grow.

When I was in the valley experience, I heard a lot of people talking about hope. But I never intentionally practiced hope.

Are you willing to let go of pain, stop defending your case, and intentionally practice hope?

If still not convinced, ask yourself this question: Where have you learned your greatest life lessons, on the mountaintop, or in the valley?

You are ready to face some enemies. No more justifications. Now is the time to take a step toward hope.

Chapter 8

STEPPING FORWARD

Let's revisit the definition of hope.

*Hope is a quality of every human spirit that places
a transformative demand upon our heart to believe
for the absolute best outcome.*

Hope is not passive, stagnant, and transient. It produces feelings but is not a feeling. Hope is active, dynamic, and transformative. Once hope is elevated from the basement of wishful thinking to a purposeful life-changing quality, it becomes easier to see how hope can change an attitude—and change a life.

In view of this definition, how would the quality of your life change if you started being intentional about hope?

How would your life change if:

1. You acknowledge that the quality of hope already exists within you?

2. You adjust your thinking that hope can transform?

3. You activate choices to produce better outcomes?

Study the three statements above. Note the demand being placed on you to do something. Rather than waiting to "see how we feel about it" we take action.

A friend of mine was a very successful Division I college football coach, even turning the University of Tulsa around in the early 2000s before continuing his career at Louisville and LSU. When Steve Kragthorpe was on our staff at Texas A&M he told me what he taught his players during his tenure as Quarterbacks Coach for the Buffalo Bills.

Coach Kragthorpe said in the midst of the chaotic crises and brutality of an NFL football game, he taught his players to adapt, adjust, and overcome.

Adapt. Adjust. Overcome.

The coach's words serve as both an excellent parallel and working mandate for how to intentionally work hope into our lives.

Adapt. You can't adapt to a situation until you first acknowledge that the situation is real and is affecting you. Now you have a choice. Do nothing, or adapt to the reality.

Adjust. If you keep thinking the same thoughts, but hope for a different outcome, you perpetuate insanity. The only way you can commit to adapting to making different choices is to adjust your thinking. This means you consider other possibilities. You dare to dream. You dare to imagine that your life could be better.

Overcome. Overcoming means you must take action. Something must be activated. You must do something. You've acknowledged there's a problem. You've adjusted your thinking to address the issue. Now, you must follow through. This is called purposeful living. Living with intention.

Nineteenth century English Pastor, F. B. Meyer, once noted there are three kinds of people:

- Some have no intention
- Some have double intentions
- Some have intentions that are pure and simple

My fervent hope is we will be intentional in our pure and simple quest to improve our lives!

What would happen in your soul if you dedicated a few minutes each day to hope?

This is how you get out of the desert. One small step at a time. One creative thought at a time. As a matter of fact, if you aren't making a conscious demand on your heart and mind to believe for the best outcome, you're not hoping, you're merely wishing.

Hope is an intentional lifestyle. This means we must replace one set of behaviors with another. If this sounds like work, it is.

Are you ready?

Living with hope

If you're in the valley, but at least pointed in the direction of the promised land, take a few minutes to see beyond your circumstances and believe there will be a good outcome.

I know it sounds almost impossible. We've been so uneducated about what hope truly is, our hope muscles have atrophied. And we're so distracted we've almost lost the ability to focus. We've replaced hope with fleeting emotion and passive wishing.

Do you want meaning and purpose? Everyday intentionally pursue exercising the muscle of hope. Once this becomes your priority, your capacity for hope will grow. Think of this as an exercise class for hope.

Okay, class. We're going to start with the most basic move—moving out of negativity by placing a demand on our hearts and minds. You have hope inside you, even if you haven't used your hope muscles in years.

Here's where we begin. Breathe in.

Yes, I'm hurting.
I never imagined I'd be in this situation.
Honestly, I wish I could just wake up from this nightmare.
This is my life right now.
But.
Circumstances might not change, but I can change.
Something good can come out of this.
I can grow from this.
I can choose to grow closer to God.
I can choose to look beyond my own emotions, and even my own life.
This has been taken away.
But so much can be restored and renewed.
Something good will come out of this.
I can be an agent of hope to others.

If you think about it, many of the "I" statements we use when we're going through a tough time are already taking us toward acknowledgement.

For example, "I'm hurting," or "I never would have imagined this nightmare," may seem inconsequential, but those statements actually highlight an inescapable reality.

Doing something about that reality is another issue. Despite the difficulty of the hour, you do have a choice as to how you will proceed!

I have a choice

You don't have to make self-destructive choices. You can intentionally look beyond what you think, what you see, and what you feel.

In a shallow, superficial culture, we react to what we see and hear. But aren't we more than just flesh and blood? Yes. We're spirit as well. And in every human spirit, there is a seed of hope. The hope in you is waiting for you to acknowledge it, and make a demand upon it, with the creative ability God gave you.

Remember Coach Kragthorpe's instruction to his NFL quarterbacks: *adapt, adjust, overcome.* Right now, I am placing a demand upon you to do something.

Resist the temptation to remain idle in the valley. The most difficult move for me was … to move—to do something. Remaining idle meant I didn't have to face the reality of the day or the uncertainty of the future. I could merely exist, which I did for months. In fact, when someone suggested "move," it literally went in one ear and out the other.

So, why should I expect you to do anything different? Because you're already miles ahead of where I was. And you're investing in your heart.

Are you ready for more?

1. How do I change my mind-set? (adapt)
2. What can you do, think, or say to improve your life? (adjust)
3. When can I implement a strategy to change? (overcome)

Changing your mind-set is a learned behavior that I've practiced for two decades. While there are many successful methods, I've followed a simple prescription offered by Frank Outlaw. Consider his words:

Watch your thoughts, they become words.

Watch your words, they become actions.

Watch your actions, they become habits.

Watch your habits, they become character.

Watch your character, for it becomes your destiny.

What if, for just five minutes a day, while in the midst of the valley, you thought of everything you were thankful for. Next, throughout the day, use words to express your thanks. That's it.

Here's the strategy. Right now—for the next five minutes—write down what you are thankful for:

_____

_____

_____

Next, look at the words you've used, and make mention of those words throughout the remainder of this day. Simply speak them. That's it. Nothing more.

During his acceptance speech to the National Football League Hall of Fame, all-pro running back, Emmitt Smith revealed invaluable wisdom learned from a high school coach. The coach told the young running back:

It's only a dream until you write it down, and then it becomes a goal.

You'll be surprised how your brain reacts to seeing words of gratitude on paper.

You'll be amazed how your mood will change as you begin using those words out loud. You'll move forward faster as you transition from writing words of gratitude to having new goals and behaviors.

Kragthorpe: *Adapt, Adjust, Overcome.*

Smith's Coach: *It's only a dream until you write it down, and then it becomes a goal.*

These two steps—as small as they may seem—are intentional choices that help your heart exit the valley.

To reinforce this notion, consider what the founder of retail giant J. C. Penney once said: "Give me a store clerk with a goal, and I will give you a person who makes history. Give me a person with no goals, and I will give you a store clerk." The statement is not an indictment against store clerks, but a menacing warning to those who take goals lightly. And, if you are really serious about experiencing change, you're willing to go to that next step of intentionality by writing down your goals. Let's give it a try.

Write down just one hope-goal. Before you do, here's a reminder of our definition:

Hope is a quality of every human spirit that places
a transformative demand upon our heart to believe
for the absolute best outcome.

Your goal should state an expected behavior you wish to accomplish. Consider this example:

I choose one time today to think of something or someone I can be thankful for.

This is powerful. Your ears heard it, now your eyes see it. You've instructed your brain to think a certain way. You have placed a demand upon your heart to hope by stating your gratitude.

Ready? Write your goal now and look at it several times today. What do you have to lose?

_____

_____

_____

Enemies of hope

One significant life-changing lesson the valley taught me was this: Growth requires discomfort. Do not expect change without being uncomfortable. This may be a hard sell in a culture that *insists* on comfort. But, the promise of hope comes with the promise of a fight—a fight against enemies that built a wall between you and hope.

The question is not how bad do you want hope. The question is, How committed are you to the fight for hope?

It's worth the fight because the battle is winnable. The key is to recognize your enemies and remove them. With that in mind, here are some enemies of hope to identify and eliminate.

Lack of trust

Following Trina's passing, I had difficulty trusting anyone, including God. I still loved God, but questioned how He could allow my wife, and my boys' mom, to die.

I see now that a lack of trust destroyed my hope and crippled my aspirations to improve my life. If you don't trust, then how can you hope? If you don't have hope, then faith—*the substance of all things hoped for*—becomes impossible to possess. Without trust there's no hope. If you have no hope, then how can you dream or imagine a better life for yourself? I was in a vicious cycle of despair, fueled largely by my lack of trust.

A lack of trust thus becomes an enemy of hope. Not trusting doesn't just rob the individual of hope, it fosters poor choices. I placed no trust in the words of others that my situation would improve. I placed little trust in God, despite His pleas for me to trust Him. The absence of trust meant I must fully control my life, and thus control the amount of pain I was willing to tolerate.

As a pastor, I often discover that people are stuck at this troubling intersection. After acknowledging the problem, they'll say, "Yes, but doesn't God want me to be happy," or, "I'm tired of being hurt!" As a motivational speaker, this too is where I discover many people are. They want hope and happiness, but because of past failures and disappointments, trust issues discourage their fight for hope.

These are legitimate concerns. But it's important to know who's doing the talking—hope or hurt? This is why spending just five minutes writing and talking about what you are thankful for is so powerful. In the midst of agonizing hurt that defines you twenty-four hours a day, let hope talk for five minutes.

Lack of faith

With no trust there is no hope. And since hope is the prerequisite for faith, the hopeless person sees no reason for which to be faithful.

Let's look at this scripture once again: "Now faith is the substance of things hoped for, and the evidence of things not seen" (Hebrews 11:1 NKJV).

When I was in the valley, I only saw "reality." And it wasn't pretty. I had no faith.

What I didn't realize then seems so obvious now. Just five minutes of creative exercise to imagine a different worldview can change the course of a life. I never gave myself permission to dream a more positive outcome. Thus, there was no evidence of things not seen—unless that evidence fit a victim's narrative and protected me at all cost.

Thus, a lack of faith becomes an enemy of hope. You destroy any evidence to the contrary of your pain, and entertain evidence that supports the fact that no one is to be trusted and I'm in control, and I'll never ever be hurt again. Period.

What a difference a positive choice could have made.

Dwelling on circumstances

Fixating on the present takes you backwards—and robs your future.

Often, we think if we're not moving forward we're remaining neutral. However, because time marches on, and because other people move on, those who are stuck are actually moving backwards.

Dwelling on circumstances is a major enemy of hope because it disrupts forward progress. *Harvard Business Review* conducted a study years ago designed to discover what increased satisfaction and emotional stability of employees. Employee satisfaction was not primarily correlated to raises, incentives, recognition, or even more time off, but rather when employees sensed progress was made—when they sensed forward momentum.

Humans are designed to look forward and move forward. When you align your heart, mind, and actions with God's design, you'll be able to hope again.

Anger

Dwelling in the valley meant I could justify my anger. Over and over.

You see, the problem wasn't me. The problem was that God allowed Trina to die. The problem was, nothing the doctors did prevented her from dying. The problem was people's words weren't helping. The problem was that the house was too big and too lonely. The problem was I hated my life!

I was angry. I was angry at the couple across the restaurant laughing as they shared dinner. I was angry with the colleague who just returned from vacation with enough pictures to fill a photo album. I was mad at the precious old couple sitting on a park bench enjoying one another as they listened to the birds sing. I was even mad at the birds for singing! I was seething with anger, which led me to develop a deep resentment for life based on what I considered to be unwarranted circumstances.

It's impossible to be angry and hopeful at the same time. Time to try something different.

Fear

When you've been through something horrible, it's natural to be fearful that something bad will happen again. It sounds like this: *Well, God, if You took her, You'll probably take one of my kids.*

This is a hard one to talk about because I haven't overcome it. Allow me to fast forward from the valley of 1996-1997, to a mountaintop of 2017.

My life with Janet, our four sons and grandchildren, is nothing short of miraculous.

However, if Janet or one of our boys is late, my worry becomes obsessive. Our two older sons are married to wonderful women who are like daughters to me. And then there's every parent's crown jewels— grandchildren! I fight fear every day in order to hope for the best for each of them.

The fear is very real and looms large. Fear is an ever-present enemy to hope. When Janet has routine physicals, I become physically ill. I will always be grateful for my friend Randy Wimpy, who sat with me for hours a few years back in a College Station hospital waiting room while my wife had a hysterectomy. I was in a panic the entire time.

I am learning—note the present tense—that trust is an ongoing class I'll be enrolled in for a lifetime. When you've experienced trauma, the question, "What if" can play a prominent role in your thinking. I'm learning how to adapt, adjust, and overcome. When those *what if's* enter my mind, I revert to favorite scriptures I say aloud. Here's my favorite:

"Finally, brethren, whatever is true, whatever is honorable, whatever is right, whatever is pure, whatever is lovely, whatever is of good repute, if there is any excellence and if anything worthy of praise, dwell on these things. The things you have learned and received and heard and seen in me, practice these things, and the God of peace will be with you" (Philippians 4:8-9 NASB).

As a Christian pastor, I highly recommend the Bible. But, feel free to use other materials that help you replace fear. Just don't give in to the *what if's!*

Fear is an enemy of hope because it paralyzes forward momentum. Fear reminds us of our hopelessness when we need to become more aware of exciting possibilities. The battle is in the mind. The battle can be overcome. Dare to think of a more positive outcome. Say it aloud. Write it down. Believe it. Hope for it.

Regret

I spent months trying to settle the score. And years regretting it. *Oh man, I wish I hadn't made those choices.*

When I looked in the mirror, I saw regret. And it was keeping me from hope.

Instead, I could've been asking, *What's my next move? What are You trying to show me, God?*

During my walk through the valley, I lost years. Just like the children of Israel in the wilderness. The trek should have taken a couple of months at most. But it took them forty years.

Whenever we're not happy with ourselves, we lash out. Then, looking backwards, we regret it. Then we repeat the cycle over and over.

We walk in circles, just going through the motions. Think about how many people are living nonproductive lives. Why? They haven't reconnected with how easy it is to hold hope.

As destructive and vicious as these enemies are, we haven't faced the giant yet.

The giant enemy of hope

The biggest enemy of hope is also the most difficult to stare down.

This giant is an attitude—a worldview many of us adopt without even knowing it. It masks itself as righteous indignation, self-care, and justice. But it can be described in one short sentence: *Life is all about me.*

It's been said, *It's your attitude not your aptitude that determines your altitude.* How true! But here's the problem. Changing my attitude from victim to overcomer destroys my comfort.

Get into the head of a widower for a moment.

I've just endured the worst thing a man can experience: the loss of his wife. My boys have just experienced the worst thing a child can know: the loss of a mommy. Why in the world would I choose an attitude that would force me to deal with the blunt-force devastation of that reality? My *it's all about me* attitude became my protector—my adrenaline.

- My attitude took into account how I felt
- My attitude consoled and comforted me
- My attitude catered to my fragile emotional state
- My attitude justified the fact that if I didn't protect and preserve myself who would?

My greatest enemy of hope was an attitude that I thought protected me. My attitude meant I didn't have to hope, have faith, change, or be challenged to grow. After all, *I tried that stuff the previous six years while a wife battled cancer, and look where it got me!*

I'm ashamed to write this but that's exactly how I operated. I became so sick of books that offer shallow clichés and clever sayings as a way to change your state of mind. Here's the truth: I didn't want my state of mind changed—I wanted my life changed!

Never once during this season in life did I hear or read any words about the power of hope.

Hope. For just five minutes, dare to imagine what might happen if your attitude changed. Just five minutes today. And try again tomorrow.

Then try for a few more days. If you're making forward progress, write down what your heart is saying.

That's enough for now.

I just wonder, what might've happened had I read some words like these? I hope you'll tell me how real hope helps you!

Taking the high ground

I want to place a demand upon you right now.

I dare you to hope. You know the difference between hope and a wish. Call forth that quality residing within you that's crying out for a better life. You see, despite my horrific attitude, something was screaming, "help" inside my soul. My attitude made it convenient to avoid the pleas, but they were there. And I bet it's the same with you.

I want you to see hope as active, dynamic, and transformative. In other words—if you can shift for just five minutes from "why me" to "what if" your spirit will explode with unexpected energy. Try it.

This is how hope will change you and your situation.

All right God, You let me down.
All right people, you disappointed me.
All right circumstances, you discouraged me.

Then hope says, *Why don't I make an effort, just for five minutes, to move past how I'm feeling? Why not imagine the best possible outcome and move toward that?*

Cultivating hope

Back in 1996, I was preparing for Trina's funeral. Dwight Edwards, my mentor and the man who stirred up hope when I needed it most, said to me, "I need her Bible."

"I don't want you to have Trina's Bible. It's *tattered* and falling apart."

Tattered. I don't recall ever using that word in reference to a Bible. But for some reason, on that particular day, I did.

"Reviewing her Bible will give me insights into Trina's walk with God," Dwight responded. "Her Bible will tell me things you can't tell me."

"But the pages are coming out. The binding's coming off. It's tattered."

"Give me the Bible, Rick," he replied with a knowing smile.

One of the only things I remember about the funeral service was Dwight holding Trina's ragged Bible, and saying, "This is her Bible. It's worn out. Pages are yellow. The binding is coming off. It's tattered. But it was that great British soulwinner, Charles Spurgeon, who said on one occasion, *"A tattered Bible is evidence of a life that is not."*

Hope requires that you believe in something more than you can produce yourself.

Whether you believe in God or not, hope is a gift from Him. Whether you're mad at God or not, He wants you to enjoy hope. Because I want you to cultivate hope, I must tell you the truth: Hope requires that you believe in something more than you can produce on your own.

It's hard to be hopeless and hopeful at the same time.

At the time of Trina's funeral, I never realized the magnitude of the Spurgeon quote. But when framed together with Dwight's comments in the parking lot of the hospital the night Trina passed, my hope was in front of me the entire time. My attitude was blocking it.

That horrible night, Dwight said, "Rick, I don't know why Trina died, but I know God is sovereign." At the funeral a few days later, holding Trina's Bible, Dwight quoted Spurgeon who said, "A tattered Bible is evidence of a life that is not."

I have thought about those two statements for two decades and have come to this conclusion. First, I had to believe in a power greater than me. I couldn't fix me because as a self-centered person my *fix* would cater to my feelings, emotions, comfort, and pain.

Second, Trina died filled with hope.

Until the moment she passed, she hoped. I know this because of those priceless and tender final conversations. And because that same tattered Bible is in my bookcase within arm's length of my desk. And every time I open that Bible—through the tears—I read her words in the margin. Hope. Despite her circumstances, hope. Despite how she may have felt physically, hope. Despite what the doctor's report may have indicated, hope. Even despite the fact that the time to call Hospice had come, hope.

If a dying woman can cultivate hope, then what's my excuse?

Chapter 9

THE POWER
YOU DIDN'T
KNOW YOU HAD

The power of hope is within your grasp.

The basics of hope are very doable.

Everywhere I go, people cry when I tell my story. I'm not just talking about churches. I'm talking about company leaders from Nike to Volkswagen of America. Regardless of whether you're a billion-dollar global giant, or a faculty of teachers in southern Iowa, everybody is going through something. My story connects, with either their pain, or their hope.

It's one thing to cry. But after the tears, it's quite another thing to place a demand on yourself to change. You've always had a seed of hope inside, and now you have the tools to help you live a lifestyle of hope.

The more you work the tools of hope, the more positive momentum you'll have in your life.

Based on the thousands of people I've interacted with, hope lies dormant in most of us. This is the reason I wrote this book—to awaken your hope.

One of my mentors, Bishop Joseph Garlington, Sr., is more than a prince of preachers and an internationally known worship leader. He is among the most thoughtful and introspective people I know. I recall him saying to me on one occasion, "Leaders are cornered." In other words, most are thrust into leadership because of circumstances that demand immediate and decisive responses.

Hope demands an immediate and decisive response.

I remember one of the best football games I've ever been associated with, the Big 12 Championship game between Texas A&M and heavily-favored Kansas State in 1998. If we won, we'd be Big 12 champions and likely play in a highly-ranked bowl game. If undefeated Kansas State won, they'd have a shot to play for a national championship. Going into that game, Kansas State was ranked Number One in the Coaches' poll with an impressive 11-0 record.

Kansas State dominated the first half of that football game. They executed flawlessly. We did not. At halftime, we were losing 17-6. Things were not looking good. And although the Wildcats—led by amazing quarterback Michael Bishop—continued adding to their lead in the second half, something happened in our locker room at halftime that encouraged us to intensify the fight.

Our head coach, R. C. Slocum, gave one of the best motivational talks ever (and I'd heard plenty of great ones from him as his chaplain and Life Skills coordinator). Suffice to say, Coach Slocum placed a demand upon players, coaches, and staff that required immediate and decisive action.

We could not just play the second half. We had to change our expectations. We had to expect a better outcome. We had to hope.

Hope demands an immediate and decisive response.

We won the game in double overtime. Final score: Texas A&M 36, Kansas State, 33.

On New Year's Day 1999, we played Ohio State in the Sugar Bowl and lost 24-14, much to the satisfaction of my wife's family—all from Ohio, and huge Buckeye fans.

But hope was not lost in defeat. Hope was sparked in the Big 12 Championship game before the Sugar Bowl. Hope was ignited when Coach Slocum demanded an immediate and decisive response from his players.

I wear that Big 12 Championship ring to this day because of what happened that night in 1998. The lesson hope ignited in my spirit was so profound I teach it as a business principle worldwide:

Don't look at the scoreboard. Just play the next play.

In other words, worry less about the outcome of the situation. Rather, focus on setting a goal that will help you overcome an enemy of hope.

Because hope demands an immediate and decisive response.

The crisis never leaves an individual in the same condition. However, it's in this uneven season of paralyzing uncertainty where the possibility exists for true leadership to emerge. Two great examples include General Dwight Eisenhower and Martin Luther King, Jr.

As commander of the Allied Forces in World War II, General Eisenhower ordered "Operation Overlord" that stormed the beaches of Normandy. Many lives were at stake. This invasion included four thousand ships, eleven thousand planes, and nearly three million soldiers from all branches of the military. If Normandy failed, the Allied troops would be forced into full retreat.

The invasion, known as "D-Day" proved successful, opening Europe to the Allies and resulted in Germany's surrender.

The night before the Normandy invasion was certainly emotionally grueling for General Eisenhower, who submitted the following entry in his journal dated June 5, 1944:

> "Our landings in the Cherbourg-Havre area have failed to gain a satisfactory foothold and I have withdrawn the troops. My decision to attack at this time and place was based on the best information available. The troops, the air, and the Navy did all that bravery and devotion to duty could do. If any blame or fault attaches to the attempt, it is mine alone."[6]

Hope placed a demand upon General Eisenhower for an immediate and decisive response, despite the potential for loss of life or even defeat. Igniting hope in your heart is transformative, life-changing, and powerful enough to push you beyond the limitations of fear.

As a former civil rights scholar, I studied the rhetoric of Martin Luther King and the Southern Christian Leadership Conference. Battling segregation in Birmingham in the early 60s proved to be a critical turning point for champions of desegregation.

In Birmingham, Eugene "Bull" Connor was the symbol of southern racism. He also was the chief of public safety. In 1963, when King defied a court order prohibiting a nonviolent march against segregation, he was arrested.

While King was in jail, a controversial protest strategy was developed and implemented. It called for using school children as protestors. In response to the students marching in the streets of Birmingham,

---

[6] General Dwight D. Eisenhower, June 5, 1944, Journal Entry. Copies of the diary are housed both at the Dwight D. Eisenhower Presidential Library in Abilene, Kansas, and at the National Archives in Washington, D. C. The journal entry was dated July 5, 1944. Historians generally believe that Eisenhower simply made a mistake with the month portion of the date.

Connor unleashed police dogs upon innocent children, and ordered firemen to turn their water hoses on them with a force that could knock bark off a tree.

Pictures from Birmingham were seen worldwide and embarrassed the Kennedy Administration. The perception was if President Kennedy could not control Birmingham, how would he function on a global stage?

The clash between children and authorities was covered by media outlets worldwide and eventually led to "The Birmingham Truce Agreement," a document implementing desegregation in the city.

Upon reflection, aide Andrew Young said King's decision to march when he didn't know what else to do, "was the beginning of Martin's true leadership."[7] Note well that King had been the leader of the civil rights movement since the beginning of the Montgomery bus boycott in 1955. Note further that King did not plan or implement a comprehensive strategy. He was simply cornered by the circumstances of a court order.

Despite the circumstances and even repercussions—including a violation of a court order, jail time, and public ridicule—hope placed a demand upon protestors for immediate and decisive action. Do you think it's possible to experience a better outcome today if you placed a demand upon your life to make a change?

Cornered

Leaders are cornered. And in that season of desperate crisis, the potential for the best possible outcome can emerge. Could it be the

---

[7] Enrique D. "Rick" Rigsby. "A Rhetorical Clash with the Established Order: An Analysis of Protest Strategies and Perceptions of Media Responses," Birmingham, 1963. (Ph.D. Dissertation, University of Oregon, 1990).

greatest proponent for hope is struggle? Could it be when the struggle is so intense all you can do is hope for the best?

Hope is an innate quality that we can call upon to actually believe in the best possible outcome. It's the same quality that causes a U. S. Airlines captain to land on the Hudson River after losing power in both engines.

It's the same quality that causes a 39-year old quarterback, Tom Brady, to mount the greatest fourth quarter comeback in Super Bowl History. (Sorry Atlanta Falcons fans!)

It's the same quality that causes a man fired by the company he founded to return to that company and—through the iPhone—reinvent the technical landscape of our world.

It's the same quality that resides inside of you, that can cause you to believe for a better outcome today.

Garlington's point is not only spot on, but parallels my argument: Hope requires struggle. Hope was designed and placed in you for struggle. Struggle creates the opportunity for hope.

Looking at my valley situation, and having two decades to reflect, I'm convinced it took an insurmountable crisis that I could not solve in order to activate hope!

We all have hope, but few place a creative demand on themselves to believe for the best. We all have hope, but few realize it's a choice you have the power to make. We all have hope, but—please trust me—few understand the present crisis you're living through is the very situation required to activate that hope!

Momentum

Let's face it, our excuses are weak.

We're in Chapter 9 and none of us have time for weak anymore, right? You don't see a winning boxer leaning backwards, do you? No. They're leaning forward. Are you?

If you're leaning forward, at least you can stumble forward. You're made to live forward, not backward. And trust me, I wasted a lot of time leaning back. When you're medicating yourself, you have a warped sense of time. Suddenly you look back and ten years have gone.

People in the valley often say, "How did I get here? When did this happen?" Those are time-related statements. I often hear recovering alcoholics say, "It started with one drink and the next thing you know, five years went by."

I want you to start creating momentum. Put one foot in front of the other, take a step, and breathe. For one moment, think about one area of your life that brings you joy. Imagine one scenario you could look forward to. Close the book, write down something hopeful, and place a demand on your heart and mind.

This exercise might seem futile, like trying to lift a four-hundred-pound barbell. But you'll get there. Is there any good that can come out of this day? Can you allow your mind to go there? Will you think positively—on purpose and despite the pain?

Even if there's only a little bit of hope, you're moving forward. Hope might feel foreign, or undeserved, but keep practicing hope.

Yeah, life can feel like an upstream swim. But that's where momentum comes in. Moments create momentum. Moments become minutes—and months.

Acting busy

Many people appear busy to cover their own lack of forward momentum.

As I've said before, in a shallow, superficial culture, truth is the first casualty. And what does the absence of truth promote? It promotes acting. So, we learn how to act to cover up our real thoughts and emotions—even our true hearts.

The result is a society of people who may not be productive, but spend all day doing something. That was me. Kurt Ritter, a dear friend and colleague in the Department of Communication at Texas A&M, helped me to realize that I was actively acting, but moving backward.

It was a month after the funeral, the numbness was wearing off and reality was setting in. By now, we're usually expected to be back in our routine. So, I'd arrive on campus around 9:00 a.m. My classes were back-to-back beginning at 9:45 a.m. with office hours in the afternoon.

I recall on this particular day getting to my office at the prescribed time and sitting at my desk. After a few minutes, Kurt stopped by my office, tapped me on the shoulder and said, "Why don't you go home, Rick?"

"I've got classes and office hours. I'm good," was my response.

"Go home," Kurt whispered.

I looked at my watch. To my horror, it was 5:00 p.m. Eight hours had passed in what seemed like ten minutes. I never went to class. I don't recall holding office hours. I sat at my desk—for what I thought was for ten minutes.

People in the valley have a warped sense of time. Days and weeks disappeared. I drove for miles, suddenly realizing I didn't know where I was or how I arrived there. Sometimes I stopped the car and just screamed.

I wasted so much time. But it's not a waste if I help you find hope.

Redeeming the time

Gratitude is the foundation of hope. Being thankful places a demand on your heart and mind—and helps you take back time and regain perspective.

How in the world can you maintain perspective if you're on a slippery slope? (You're in the valley, you've just been fired, just received the diagnosis, she just left you, he just died, you're in the emergency room.)

Business consultants typically agree that we are distracted daily, some argue as much as two hours per day. What would happen if we intentionally focused on just 10 percent of those 120 minutes? *For twelve minutes, despite what I know, despite what I'm feeling, even despite what I see, for twelve minutes I'm going to focus on what I can be thankful for.*

I'm not asking you for 100 percent, or even 50 percent. Your twelve minutes may be one minute today. But what can you be thankful for? That's quantifying hope.

No one shared the power of thankfulness with me. That's why I'm sharing with you. The power of active gratitude forces you to move beyond what you're feeling. It forces you to let go of the burden of being self-centered.

It's one thing to quote Bible verses about thankfulness, but if I can't make application of the verse, I've just given you another burden to carry. However, if I can put hands and feet on the verse, helping you move forward into thankfulness, you can gain momentum for your journey out of the valley.

Just one minute to think about your loved ones who are still alive makes a difference. Taking one minute to consider the blessing of where you live or work will build momentum. A minute to find what's right with your world can change your world.

But if all you do is read these suggestions and don't practice them, you might as well just watch television. I say that because, decades ago, I would've given anything to hear about the mechanics of hope.

I can't tell you how many times people have come up to me and said, "Your speech gave me hope." What are they really saying? *Your speech pulled me out of the pit for just a moment.*

And *just for a moment* is where we begin.

Pursuing peace

I don't just quote the Bible because I'm a Christian. The Bible has an incredible amount of insight into our minds and emotions. From a biblical perspective, you learn your mind will be in perfect peace if it remains on God.

You will keep him in perfect peace, whose mind is stayed on You, because he trusts in You (NKJV).

Isaiah wrote this almost three thousand years ago in Isaiah 26:3.

My modern reconstruction of that sentence is this: If you can force your mind to think on something other than you or your circumstances, you've just increased the likelihood of developing a peaceful mind.

When we focus on ourselves we tend to lose our peace; it's not a healthy perspective. When we gaze inward, we lose forward momentum. And if it's all about us, peace can't exist. I would argue that most people with a victim mentality don't have peace because of this tempting mind-set. Listen to their language.

"Woe is me. I got fired. It wasn't fair. I hate that person."

Well, what might happen to your level of peace if you focused on someone other than yourself? And what if this someone was God?

Wondering

I wonder … Do you?

Wondering is a form of creativity, and like all creative power, can be used positively or negatively.

I wonder if I will ever be happy again … versus, *I wonder what good can come out of this situation.*

Or more profoundly:

I wonder why that person is such a jerk, versus, *I wonder how I can encourage them.*

Wondering is a form of meditation—not in the sense of Eastern religion's practice of meditation, but a form of intentional thought that's so simple, our busy culture has squeezed it out of our lives. Meditating is simply thinking about something on purpose, for an extended period of time.

What's *an extended period of time?* Exactly one minute longer than your restless mind wants to.

Loss and gains

I always benefitted from the day after the loss of a football game at Texas A&M.

We won a lot of games, but the day after a loss was really eye-opening. The nature of college football is you don't have much time to wallow in your own pity. Even though Alabama beat you last week, Mississippi is coming next week.

The day after a loss, you look at the videotape with the sole purpose of seeing what your mistakes were and how you can rectify those mistakes to develop a plan for the next opponent.

What would happen if we practiced that in life?

Instead of saying, "Look what the opponent did to me! I can't believe it!" what if we coached ourselves to say, "What can I do to learn from the past, look to the future, and move toward the best possible outcome?"

To keep moving forward, start asking yourself some hard questions.

Am I responsible for any of this? Maybe, or maybe not. Am I accountable for my reaction? Yes. Am I responsible for my own happiness, for my joy, for my peace? Yes.

Maybe it's not your fault. Maybe it's nobody's fault. Despite where the fault lay, is there something I can learn by realistically looking at where I am? The question then becomes, why is it most people don't want to recognize where they are? From my perspective, it's simply too painful. We're afraid to hope.

In 1996, all I saw was loss. My reality was, *I'm a widower at forty years of age. I have two children who don't have a mother.*

Who wants to face that reality? I'd much rather look at a full schedule and a medium-rare steak. But there was more to my reality. More possibility for love than I imagined, and more capacity to help people than I ever dreamed. I had a choice. You have a choice.

Right now, we can make a simple choice to acknowledge there's good available if we keep moving forward. And here's another wonderful choice we have. We can water the seed of hope in others by reminding them of these truths.

Endangered species

In 2015, I was sitting in a restaurant in McKinney, Texas, trying hard to pretend I wasn't overhearing the nearby conversation. But I was so intrigued I even shifted my seat closer to the two men and a lady talking.

After about five minutes of stealth eavesdropping, the topic became clear. Two prominent figures in a church were grilling this woman, who had left the congregation. They wanted to know why, and she won the argument with one phrase.

"I would buy into your belief system, but I can't get past your behavior."

I almost dropped my fork. They continued talking, but I was suddenly aware of my own need to put my beliefs into action—a lifestyle. Why are our churches not leading the way when it comes to being agents of hope? Because people haven't led the way. Because I haven't led the way. And in the absence of our churches leading the way, it's not a surprise people seek comfort in drugs, alcohol, pornography, materialism, work, and food.

Why is politics not leading the way in hope? Why is your business not leading the marketplace in hope? These questions expose the fact that society has made hope a separate and discreet notion from its original intent.

Hope's original intent was to be a motivating factor to inspire the heart.

We've strayed. And as a result, our society has strayed. I would argue one of the greatest dwindling commodities in this world is a hope-filled person. I would even say one of the dwindling commodities in church is a hope-filled member, and in business, a hope-filled individual.

Agents of hope

In my experience, so few are trained to be agents of hope. You and I can stir up hope in people. But it takes knowledge and courage.

It's not "normal" to say to someone in the valley, "I know you're struggling, Rick. And I can't even imagine what you're going through. But today, take one minute and think of what you can be thankful for. I'll check on you tomorrow."

But introducing true hope is so much better than cheap imitations like, "She's in a better place," or "I know just how you feel. My dog died last month."

My favorite professor in graduate school had some poignantly profound parting words for me. "Be incredibly competent in your research, preparation, and teaching. And be kind to your students."

I was blessed to win awards at Texas A&M because of one reason: Yeah, I was a pretty good teacher, but I was an even better agent of hope. Even my failing students had hope. (Although I suspect they were putting all their hope on summer break.) The only ones that didn't have hope were those who refused to cultivate it.

I remember teaching at Fresno State when a student came to my office and informed me that his parents had been involved in an accident. He asked if he could reschedule his final exam. I was heartbroken. I told the student he could take the exam any time, but encouraged him that his first responsibility was caring for his family. I believed I gave this student hope despite his circumstances. I was kind. I was an agent of hope.

The next day, the same student walked into my office and told me he made the entire story up so he wouldn't have to take a test he was not prepared for.

I gave the student an F right on the spot. I believe this too gave the student hope! I listened to his tearful justification, and saw a repentent heart. However, he lied. He cheated. And he would have to pay the consequences.

Here comes the hope. He learned a critical life lesson: *It is never wrong to do the right thing.* You may not think so, but receiving a failing grade on an exam is a small price to pay for a lesson that has the potential to keep you out of prison.

You don't have to be degreed or undergo special training to be an agent of hope. Simply encourage people to look less at the circumstances and more at the opportunities to move forward. It takes courage. Show them by relating a story from your own experience. You will be amazed by how people respond once you place a kind demand upon them.

By the way, I hope that Fresno State student is reading this page right now. I would love to hear how you're using that minor setback to encourage hope in others!

Choose to be an agent of hope. We all have the capacity to enhance, brighten, empower, encourage, energize, and bless people.

I know what you're thinking. *I don't want to get involved in someone else's life.* I used to worry about that, too. But then, I was in a place where I could not find hope. And, I would have given anything to hear or see hope from somebody. I've never gotten over this. In fact, my favorite part of every speaking engagement occurs off stage. Don't get me wrong, I love speaking. But my favorite part is projecting hope in my eyes without saying a word. Let me explain.

For many years, I was not the one on the stage but rather in the audience. I was sitting in my seat, broken, dejected, and disillusioned. My thinking was, *If I could just get close to the speaker and perhaps see hope in that person, maybe … there might be hope for me, too.*

I have never forgotten what it was like to be that person in the crowd. In fact, much to the consternation of my family, I love being the last person to leave an auditorium. I recall one event in North Carolina a few years back, when the band that performed prior to me speaking had packed up all the instruments, loaded them in the trailer behind their bus, and were walking out of the venue while I was still talking to people.

Do you know how long it takes for a band to pack up? My boys were not particularly fond of Dad that night!

I want to shake every hand, sign every book, and hug every person. I want to be a visual representation of a person once-discouraged and brokenhearted, who dared to push past fear to find hope.

Here's the point. Start becoming an agent of change right now. Don't be afraid to use what you got to help people get what they need!

Zig Ziglar was really on to something when he said, "Achieve your goals by helping others achieve theirs."

Do you have a friend, coworker, or family member who needs some truth, spoken in love? Point them in the direction of hope.

I have decided to make hope a lifestyle, a mind-set, a way of living life. Life is lived in coffee shops and ball fields. Life is lived in hospital waiting rooms and corporate offices. My friend Dwight pastors a church in a Houston suburb. His requirement for all members of his staff: You must have a part-time job away from the church. I love this. You know what Dwight is doing? Releasing people to go into the community where hurting people are, and be agents of hope.

I guarantee you that today you will encounter at least one person who feels hopeless. And regardless of whether you're in a valley or a mountaintop, make a choice to be the difference in someone's life.

The power of hope resides within you. Live it. Use it. Share it!

Chapter 10

FREEDOM

Originally, the working title for this book was, *An Empty Closet and a Tattered Bible*. During my valley experience, I allowed my emotions and feelings to control me. The results were devastating. Physically, I was overweight. Emotionally, I was unhealthy. And spiritually, I was a Christian with more questions than answers. My closet was cluttered with the results of impulsive purchasing designed to medicate my pain. That closet became a metaphor for a heart filled with useless, destructive emotions.

When I was "cornered" by my wife and challenged to look realistically at my life, I realized that my closet needed cleaning.

After Trina died, I also made another discovery. I realized that her Bible was tattered. For years, I contemplated the dynamically uneven intersection of an empty closet and a tattered Bible only to conclude that both could put me on a pathway to discovering hope.

Freedom from the physical bondage of pounds and clothes that no longer fit proved to also be a spiritual exercise. For the first time in my life, after nearly a half a decade, I felt I was being set free. One by one, emotions I felt I "had" to carry were leaving. Clothing I felt I couldn't survive without was disappearing. Associations and assumptions I did not think I could live without were no longer necessary. Finding the courage to hope was cleaning my closet from the accumulation of decades of stuff that was harmful and useless.

But as my heart and mind became less cluttered, I made room to believe. I began the day by stating:

This is the day that the Lord has made, and I will be glad. My joy is not contingent upon whether I'm married or single. And even though I'm having a hard time with this, I'm going to make a choice to think this way for at least ten minutes.

Eleanor Roosevelt said that we ought to "do something every day that scares us." For me, it was eating kale!

But seriously, it's a very scary thing to venture forth with no partner, no future, no hope. Doing something that scared me was attempting to face a day without medicating. The time had come to leave the safe zone of distractions and try to live again. But I wondered how.

1. Acknowledgment that my life is out of control.
2. Making a choice to reverse the spiral.
3. Moving from choice to action.

What if I told you that a dying wife taught me how to live? As I've shared Trina's story before audiences throughout the world—both in corporate and church settings—something resonates with audiences. In fact, throughout the years of public speaking, the subject of an empty closet generates the biggest response.

Inside the closet of her heart was love, trust, and hope. She had a love for God and people that was unparalleled. And, to the very end, she had hope that she would be the next miracle to survive breast cancer. And, although it was not to be, Trina gave me a glimpse of hope rarely seen. Time was not spent anguishing over lost opportunities or even the looming possibility of shortness of days. Energy was not exerted gossiping about people or complaining. People in critical condition have little time or tolerance for grudges. And, never—not once—did I hear Trina lose hope. She simply did not—even though I believe she knew she was dying, she didn't lose hope.

What I'm reporting is nothing short of a miracle.

Moments are miracles

There weren't long nights of crying or days filled with sadness. This is not to say there weren't moments. We had many. But, while my tendency was to dwell on the sorrow, that wasn't the case for Trina. Inside her closet weren't many excess emotions. She was practical and real and full of faith. Trained as a registered nurse, she was acutely aware of stage-four cancer, and did all she could to survive, while trusting for a miracle until the very end. For Trina, her closet was free of emotional baggage—excess hurts and regrets over what could've been.

Often, hope surfaces in the incongruities of life. For example, how could a dying person have hope for a miracle and a long life? I've had two decades to reflect and have come to this conclusion. For Trina, it really wasn't about the outcome. She knew she would die. Everyone will die. And because she believed in Christ, she knew she would have eternal life. Trina wasn't living for the outcome. Her hope was in the journey. Some of her last words to me were:

It doesn't matter to me any longer how long I live.
What matters most … is how I live.

Could it be that we spend so much time in the future that there is always a hope deferred? Tomorrow wasn't promised to Trina. Only that day. Only that hour. Only that moment. The length of life—something that consumes us and distracts us—was not her focus. Her hope rested in how she would live.

Aware until the very end that her sons and husband were not just comforting but watching her, Trina's closet and tattered Bible gave her hope—one moment at a time. Without need or want of a spotlight, a dying woman taught us how to live, and how to hope—moment by moment.

Filling your closet with hope

Let me encourage you to empty your closet of all unnecessary baggage that keeps you from discovering hope. Now you have the space, and the room to fill your heart with hope.

So, what did I learn? My hope is usually associated with a desired outcome yet to happen. Rarely, if ever, is my hope grounded in now. Right now, this moment can be a joyous one—if I acknowledge, choose, and act.

Listen carefully as people describe what they're hoping for. Don't you find it interesting, that for most, hope is described as an event yet to come? And, don't you find it ironic that those who chose to live in the moment, and discover the hope contained in that moment, seem to be more grounded and more at peace?

There is something to be said for living in the moment. I enjoy life the most when I stay in the moment. For me, this means not allowing my past failures to trigger memories and affect my peace of mind. This means not looking ahead and making a choice to worry about variables that I cannot control.

Living in the moment is contentment for me. It is resting in the assurance that I am doing my best to fulfill my purpose. This lifestyle instructs my heart to believe for the best possible outcome. It creates the capacity for hope to ignite and reside in spaces once occupied by fear and worry and anger.

I love an empty closet. It's a good thing. Why? Empty creates space for a refill.

Emptying my closet of destructive habits and filling it with hope was a critical turning point in my life. I no longer choose to make time or use energy for destructive behaviors that once filled my closet. Such new behaviors agitate the enemies of hope and encourage them to live and breathe in your heart. At all cost, avoid the following agitators from lodging in your closet:

Jealousy

For many months, I was jealous of anyone who had a relationship—even a dysfunctional one. As long as they were together, they represented something I was not. Instead of making a choice to celebrate a couple, feelings of envy tried to crowd my mind. Anything that removed this emotion became a welcomed distraction and constant companion.

Pride

Pride kept returning to my closet. Years earlier, I made a decision that nobody was going to tell me what to do. After all, I trusted doctors and they let me down, or so I reasoned. Self-preservation was my lifestyle.

The opposite of pride is trust. I needed to trust that I may not have all the answers, but I might need to get some help and let go of some control.

Think about the arguments you've had with your spouse or with others close to you. Is the argument productive or is it based on pride and self-preservation?

Pride, not trust, became a constant in my life. When you're at rock bottom, you don't see the severe consequences of a prideful life. Not only does pride retard one's ability to trust, but from a spiritual perspective, it places a bull's eye on your back.

Consider the words of Jonathan Edwards: *"Nothing sets a person out of the Devil's reach as humility."*

The problem with ego is the one afflicted is generally the last one to learn of the condition. The great danger is not limited to the prideful individual, but to those they interact with. When your life is marked by pride, you live a shallow existence born out of insecurity and everyone around you suffers. When life is all about you, your life will bear the fruit of constant complaining, a lack of gratefulness, and a self-righteous arrogance that pushes people away, abuses relationships, misuses opportunities to serve, and refuses to acknowledge the need for anything—especially God. And so you live life in an alternative reality, constructed in large measure due to a lack of trust that compels you to self-preserve, self-protect, and self-medicate. Pride becomes a regular roommate for the suffering person.

Confusion

Any time your environment is changed or threatened, there will be confusion. Change produces tension and can create confusion. All great innovations begin with tension—whether you're lifting weights or disrupting the marketplace. But guess where we often remain? We stay stuck in the tension, and that's where confusion reigns. We become confused about our identity, our role, and confused by our emotions.

These agitators linger and have the power to breathe life into the enemies of hope. Remember this: Hope demands an immediate and decisive response. Thus, in the face of jealousy, pride, and confusion, make a choice to expect a better outcome. A slight adjustment to your thinking can create a new beginning.

A new beginning

An empty closet is a fresh start. And it's sometimes awkward. When your mind becomes accustomed to chaos and clutter, peace and simplicity can seem both refreshing and strange.

It took just a few hours to pack the boxes of clothes and shoes, but it took years for me to pack stuff in. I had become friends with the enemies of hope. They took up residence in my life—like useless clothes in a closet. Now, the freedom of becoming untangled is liberating. And, the thought of adding dynamic, transformative, life-giving substance to that closet is pure joy—not to mention purposeful.

When I discovered hope and when I needed to regain hope, I found purpose. For half my life, I thought my purpose was to live for me, to promote me, to exalt me. Become wealthy, get ahead, be a success.

Dealing with my fear and working to climb out of the valley forced me to examine the motivations *behind* the goals. I'm embarrassed to report it was all about me. I had strayed from a fundamental lesson learned from my dad—a third-grade dropout, yet the wisest man I have ever met. He would say, "Son, God blesses you so you may help others." It would take years of being stuck at rock bottom to remind me of that lesson.

I was created and placed on this earth for one reason: to offer hope and encouragement to a hurting and hopeless world. You cannot offer what you don't have. Thus, I am more convinced than ever that,

My heart had to be broken, so I would have a heart for the brokenhearted.

The valley gave me a fresh start and clarified my purpose in life.

How could the worst days of my life be the best? You must find the courage to continue fighting if you want the answer.

I am laughing right now as I write because developing that broken heart makes for some funny moments.

I never cried until after Trina passed away. I was reared by great parents and influenced by a tough World War II and Great-Depression-surviving dad who insisted on toughness for my brother and me. I'm not sure what my dad would think about me crying so much these days!

A few years ago, one of our younger sons had a friend over. They were watching television, and my son occasionally watched me, glancing in a way that I would get the hint. The glance was code for *Dad, please leave the room*. But last I checked, it was my house too, and I was perfectly comfortable in my leather recliner. They continued to watch television, and talked in hushed tones—as if teenagers had any possible information I wanted to hear. Then, a television commercial came on. You remember the one where the dog grows with the child. When the child is young the dog is a pup, and thirty seconds later, the child is going to college and the dog is the epitome of sadness as it confronts a lonely and quiet house.

I cried for five minutes. Cried like a baby. Cried and snorted. It didn't go over well with my son and his guest. After his friend left, my son shared his embarrassment over me crying. In a rare moment of father-son clarity, I said, "I'm sorry, son. But my heart had to be broken so I'd have a heart for the brokenhearted—even a broken-hearted dog."

It was one of those rare moments where there was no arguing or challenging. My son got it. So had I. I know my purpose for being on this earth. My struggles—though massive—were a small price to pay to discover hope and purpose.

Discovering hope

Try the following initial steps to push you from hopeless to hopeful. Whether you're in a valley, or on top of the mountain, or somewhere in between, these steps will encourage you to dream of a better outcome.

1. Take inventory of your closet.

Obviously, I am speaking of your heart. This is not a time for vague generalities. Honestly list destructive behaviors and what you think the root causes might be. For example, I would lie to people when they asked, "How are you doing?" I answered, "fine" to avoid further intrusion from them. Root issue: Mistrust. I trusted nobody. *I wasn't sure I could trust you with how I really felt. So, why take a chance that someone else may hurt me?*

Take inventory right now.

_____

_____

_____

2. Live for now.

As a professor, I would often tell students to worry less about how many notes they take and more about how much they retain. I would remind them that we may not cover all the day's learning objectives, but that did not mean learning did not occur. I would challenge them to focus less on the grade and more on the lesson learned. That never went over very well.

How does this apply to your life? We are so conditioned to get to the end we often minimize the value of the journey. With two decades to reflect, I now see what I could not at rock bottom: I was hurting so badly that all I wanted was relief. What I chose not to acknowledge was that I was still living. My heart was still beating. In other words, hope was deferred because I refused to dwell in the moment.

When the moment is too painful, too mundane, or too (fill in the blank), your mind drives toward preservation and protection rather than risk and reward. Hope means forcing yourself to believe for the best possible outcome. It's hard work, but the reward is worth the risk.

The bottom line: We cannot possibly believe that hope could be contained in struggle. But the reality is—that is exactly where hope resides. Think about it this way. Your most basic, fundamental survival skills were not learned in the good times. They were learned while you were at war, in battle—those times when you're out of money, out of time, out of options.

That place called "rock bottom"—that moment or season of horrific struggle where only God can rescue you—can be the greatest classroom on earth. Consider the words of Samuel Chand in his brilliant book, *Leadership Pain: The Classroom for Growth*.

"When you interpret your pain as bigger, more important, more threatening, more comprehensive than your vision, you'll redefine your vision down to the threshold of your pain."[8]

Chand argues that we must see pain as our greatest teacher. The problem is, when you're at rock bottom, the last thing you desire is to be taught. Your chief desire is escape. And, if a physical escape is not necessary, an emotional escape that medicates becomes a suitable alternative. I never realized that the constituents of hope were all around me at rock bottom. Without the grace of God and words of real hope, never in a million years would I realize the relief I longed for and the answers

---

[8] Samuel Chand, *Leadership Pain: The Classroom for Growth*. Nashville: Thomas Nelson, Inc., 2015.

I searched for were right there, waiting for me to activate them, with a simple choice.

3. **Make a choice.**

Begin to see hope as dynamic and transformative, and above all, residing inside of you. Make a choice to place a demand upon your spirit to activate the hope within you by expecting a better outcome.

Here's a valuable lesson from the valley that I could not see in the middle of the struggle: Growth happens in the process, if we pay attention. The joy of life is in the moment, not in a worrisome possible circumstance.

My counsel is this: don't rush. You're on nobody's timetable. It's important that you not miss a step. Please allow me to give you permission to empty your closet any way you want to. You might be saying to yourself, *Rick, I think I need to spend a month on regret for ten minutes a day.*

I think that's fine. Here's the great news: You're moving in the right direction, and you'll gain momentum naturally.

There is so much power released when we make the right choice. At some point, you will begin to feel a lightness in your heart. You will start to enjoy the feeling of fewer burdens in your life. No longer will there be a desire to only preserve yourself. You'll begin to care more about others and want to be an agent of hope.

The empty closet is a journey, not a destination. The empty closet today represents a journey I plan to be on the rest of my life.

In process

In 1985, I was taping a television interview with a man who ran a drug rehab facility in Willows, California. As the camera rolled, I said,

"Bill, you're a recovered alcoholic. What's the secret?" He immediately waved his hand and stopped the interview.

"Rick, I'm not a *recovered* alcoholic. I am a *recovering* alcoholic. I lived in an outcome-oriented world—either it is or isn't, either you're recovered or you're not. Neither one is true."

I think that's what keeps many people from going to the next level. And it goes something like this: *I read the book, nothing's changed. I heard the sermon, nothing changed. I listened to the motivational speaker. Nothing's changed.*

The truth is, you're changing as you read these words whether you perceive it or not.

Have you ever sat still and watched a plant go from seed to blossom? Me neither.

One day you see a sprout, then a stem, and the next time you look there's a bud. A few days pass, and the bloom appears. Change happens, but we're usually not aware of the process in real time.

The closet never empties, friend. The world will keep trying to fill it up with garbage, and we must keep replacing the lies with truth.

In baseball, if you strike out two times in a game, but get one hit, you're going to the Hall of Fame because you'll have a 330-batting average. Don't embrace false hope which expects to hit a home run every day.

Don't be afraid to take inventory of your closet.

Don't be afraid what you may find. Stay right there. Live in the moment.

Don't be afraid to make a choice.

Place a demand upon your heart to believe for the absolute best possible outcome.

As you consider inventory, the moment, and believing the best, remember this: Your circumstances may or may not change. But the newfound hope that is fueling your heart will transform you and even challenge your perception of how you view those circumstances. It produces a healthy perspective that enriches the quality of your life.

Matt Chandler is a great pastor, dynamic teacher, and most of all committed family man and friend. But, for me, lessons he shared from his valley experience are of immense value.

Diagnosed with terminal cancer a few years ago, the Lead Teaching Pastor wrote a blog to communicate with his family, friends, and congregants at the Village Church north of Dallas. With Matt's permission, allow me to paraphrase one post that made a profound impact on me.

"Most conversations among us men are pointless and lack urgency. Most men are wooed and seduced by that which is meaningless and frivolous that doesn't amount to anything."

Matt was miraculously healed and his church is thriving. As for his quote, it's devastatingly true. Consider the average rhetorical exchanges offered by most men:

"I got a new truck."

"Oh, you did? It's big. It's shiny. I want a new truck."

"Well, let me tell you how to make it happen."

And off we go.

When you survive the valley and discover hope along the journey, you're never the same. Circumstances never leave you the same. Like Matt, it is possible to go through struggle and come out with a healthy perspective, an appreciation for life, a clear purpose for living, and a lack of tolerance for that which is nonproductive and distracts from our purpose.

The world has a way of throwing a lot of stuff toward us. There are a lot of voices and images competing for our hearts. Most of those things aren't necessarily good. Suddenly, we find ourselves wanting things that we don't need, praying for things that are not helpful, and longing for things that will set us back. But because all we can see is what we choose to see, we make poor choices to allow those things to come in our closet.

Scripture teaches to *guard your heart* (Proverbs 4:23). Remove the useless debris, and make room for the transformative power of hope. Begin expecting a better outcome.

Chapter 11

A FUTURE

What does your future look like?

If you answer, *I have no idea*, you're wrong.

We all have an idea. We might not want to admit it or face what we have in mind. Remember, our minds abhor a vacuum and will fill up on fear and denial if we don't choose hope.

In the valley, I thought I had no future—not a bright one anyway—and I resented even the suggestion that I would.

Boy, was I wrong!

A new perspective

The best thing that ever happened to me was going through the valley. For those of you reading this and going through the storm right now—please resist the temptation to throw this book out the window.

Once I worked through the layers of self, I began to see a future. I saw a future that looked nothing like my past. My present looked fantastic too. Janet, Jeremiah, Andrew, Zachary, and Joshua. Wow. Never imagined that during those first months in the valley.

Working through my agenda, my motivation, my needs, my questions (see the operative word here?) allowed me to see something other than my hurt and pain. As I began to dream, as I dared myself to believe for the absolute best possible outcome, I envisioned a future unimaginable just a few years earlier. I saw the potential to help people, to offer people words of encouragement, to lift people higher, to empower people to do great things, to challenge people to stand and not quit. I began explaining to people what I had learned—and challenged them to do the same.

I began placing a transformative demand upon their hearts to believe for the absolute best outcome.

Guess what I have discovered two decades and four million miles later?

First, we all were created with a capacity to hope. However, it is dormant in most of us. And second, 99.9 percent of the people that I encountered—from every walk of life, representing every level of life, from Africa to Asia to Europe—have one thing in common:

They want to hope.

But for various reasons—and many outlined in this book—they're afraid.

Stay with me here. We have the capacity to hope. And, we want to hope. Then where's the problem?

You got it. We are the only ones standing in the way! And that's a fixable problem. That's something within your control! (I'm shouting joyfully right now!)

Ralph Waldo Emerson nailed it when he said, "The only person you're destined to become, is the person you decide to be."

Decide

Hope is in you. Decide right now to choose hope over gloom and despair. Remember our working definition of hope. Write it down. Post it on the mirror, the refrigerator, on your computer—but get it into every fiber of your being:

> *Hope is a quality of every human spirit that places*
> *a transformative demand upon our heart to believe*
> *for the absolute best outcome.*

Choose

Have you ever been presented with an idea and your first impulse is to strongly oppose it? You resist such a notion so vehemently that your mind clicks from rational to closed in a split second? This happened to me in that initial hospital parking lot conversation right after Trina died.

Ironically, time in the valley, wallowing through an emotional minefield, and endlessly replaying my nightmare while hoping for a different outcome, were vital. My "suffering process" actually *forced* me to face a new reality. It was a reluctant choice, though a choice nonetheless.

Don't expect forward momentum to occur in your life as long as you tolerate your state of hopelessness. When I could no longer tolerate living in such vicious turmoil, anything—everything—was on the table for evaluation. I remember thinking, *something has got to kick me in the butt and jumpstart me.*

I can't pinpoint the exact time after Trina's death that the search began, but I found myself replaying conversations in my mind. Amidst thousands of words spoken by hundreds of people, only two examples impacted my senses and continued to flood my mind with a reassuring familiarity. First, were the actions of my best friend, Haywood, who would simply sit with me for hours.

While I would cry during these visits, Haywood was silent. He never said a word. I remember one night we watched TV for a few hours … but the television wasn't turned on. Silence is not only golden; silence can be a language of hope. My friend's presence spoke loudly.

What my pain didn't allow me to see or hear then, I clearly see now. Perspective.

The other standout example of hope came from my dear friend and mentor, Dwight Edward's statement that seemed so incongruent at the time. Let's take a closer look at Dwight's words to me in an effort to identify the locus of hope:

"Rick, I don't know why Trina died, but I know God is sovereign."

Dwight's words were both harsh and healing. His words represented a different reality that in the coming months would threaten my hopelessness. What caused a part of me to immediately latch on, and inevitably hold on, to those words for years?

1. **Dwight's words offered a clear picture of reality.**

In effect, my friend was saying to me, "Your answer cannot be discovered within the human realm. She died, and I cannot give you a good reason why." Medically, Trina's heart finally gave out after battling a virulent type of breast cancer which metastasized into her lymph nodes, liver, and bones—despite years of chemotherapies, surgeries, and radiation treatments.

In reflecting on those words, I've come to the conclusion that most of our words are trite and meaningless, and often—though well-intentioned—are meant to appease rather than reflect reality.

Dwight's words were not intended to soften the blow. They were a straightforward, gut-wrenching statement of reality. And, it was exactly what I needed.

"I don't know why Trina died." The reality is no human knows why. The reality is, she's gone and she is not coming back to this earth. The reality is, Trina's life on this earth was over. I could run from this reality, but I couldn't change it.

Regardless of my actions, Dwight's statement of reality was a touchstone ... a verbal benchmark that communicated, "Rick, here's the deal. Sooner or later you must confront what's real."

Right now you may be at a hopeless point. Diving into fantasy only satisfies for so long. At some point one must surface for air. That's where you see the glimmer of hope—hidden in the layers of reality.

2. **Dwight's words reinforced a solid biblical belief: God is sovereign, humans are not.**

Let me make this clear. All these years later, I still don't have the answers to the questions I once demanded God answer. I have heard every theological, logical, and illogical reason of what happened. What I do know is this: I have worked through the worst of the worst issues and can say without hesitation, *it is well with my soul.* For the valley changed my life. The valley clarified my purpose. It was in the valley where I found the courage to hope.

One word of reality

Hope was hidden in the harsh reality of undeniable truth. It was found in the word, *but.* "I don't know why Trina died, *but* I do know that God is sovereign."

Note the word "but." What a bold and revolutionary word! This little word can change a life. *But* says, "Although reality sucks right now, there is another good reality which is just as true. Do you want to know more?" In retrospect, that simple word, *but* left the door open to the possibility of better days.

He started painting a picture of future possibilities: *I know God is sovereign.* Those few simple words challenged me to consider dreaming again.

Hope helps us get unstuck, in time, and lifts our imagination into good things which lie ahead. Everyone has a vision for the future. Is your view of the future dreadful or hopeful?

The fact that I held on to those words for dear life ought to be an indication that they functioned as a future hope, despite the fact I didn't acknowledge it at the time. Hope is most accessible where you least expect to find it.

Let there be light

Words are powerful. If you're stuck in the past, you need hopeful words in your ears, and you need to speak hopeful words.

Agents of hope speak words of hope to others. Boldly. But where do we find the words? I recommend consulting the Creator of words.

I recall that God even inspired a song about hope in Scripture. I love these song lyrics. See if you know them.

I waited patiently for the LORD; he turned to me and heard my cry.
He lifted me out of the slimy pit, out of the mud and mire;
he set my feet on a rock and gave me a firm place to stand (Psalm 40:1,2).

These lyrics sound like they were written by someone who spent some time in the valley. And they were. King David wrote what we know as the first two verses of Psalm 40.

Yes, I love the hope in these words, but cringe at the first line: *I waited patiently.*

There are times in life when we need to be quiet and patient. When does confusion mount up? Often, when too many plates are spinning—and crashing. To move from the past to the future, we need to … pause.

If we stay addicted to the frenzy of activity and whirlwind of thoughts, we'll start to construct our future based on desperation. But if we pause and hope, we'll see ourselves in the plan God has for us: standing on a rock, singing another verse of Psalm 40, "Many, Lord my God, are the wonders you have done, the things you planned for us…" (v. 5).

What if?

What if we allow ourselves to dream in the middle of the valley?

What if we allowed ourselves to see more than the loss and pain?

What if you laughed again?

What if, in the midst of confusion, we saw ourselves bringing hope to people?

What if going through our problem, made us uniquely qualified to help others with their problems?

What if we allowed ourselves to ask, *What if?*

I'll tell you what would happen; your life would be transformed.

What would your life look like if you spent the next ten years being the most grateful person you know? What would your family look like? What would your career look like? What would your business look like? What would your relationships look like if you became the most hopeful person you know?

Sounds pretty rosy, right? Let's talk about it right now.

What would the rest of your day look like if you spent ten minutes being the most hopeful person you could be?

Did you just hit a brick wall?

In the valley, we often don't feel we have the right to imagine a good future. Why is that? Many people have a warped perspective that when we do things right today, we're somehow closer to God. But if we mess up tomorrow, we're far from God. In other words, God's love—and God's goodness to me in the future—is contingent upon our behavior.

And so, when we're in the valley, and mad at God, we don't feel we have the right to think differently—hopefully. We don't give ourselves permission to dream when we need it most.

It's ironic—when you feel you deserve God's help the least, that's when you need it the most.

That's when our heavenly Father wants to give grace to you. Will you give yourself permission to receive?

Permission

You play a crucial role in your future.

Sounds overly simplistic, I know. But in the valley, it's easy to forget that we still must choose. We must give ourselves permission to hope.

Giving yourself permission to imagine is simple but crucial.

For me it was, *Rick, why don't you choose to see thousands of people hearing your story and receiving hope? Why don't you imagine helping others become agents of hope?*

In 1996, I would never have given myself permission even to entertain such a conversation. When I needed it the most, I was the least receptive to the thought. Have you given yourself permission to imagine a bright future?

Like any valuable endeavor, there's work involved. In the case of dreaming, our imagine muscles need a good workout. In our society, we place fewer and fewer demands on ourselves for growth. We'd rather push a button or ask someone else.

I'm guilty, too. When I pick up my rental car, even if I'm familiar with the city, I still rely on my phone to remember how to get to my destination. Why tax my precious brain cells to plot my course?

In the valley, often there's very little expected of you. *Ain't nobody going to hold me accountable. People are too busy feeling sorry for me, and part of me enjoys it!*

How many demands do you place upon yourself to grow?

Demand hope

Your hope and your future depend on your intentional effort.

I'm not talking about struggling to keep up appearances, or working to put your game face on. I'm talking about making a demand on your heart and mind to see yourself in a better future. *I don't know exactly how, but I will laugh again, I will live again, I will love again!*

So, let me ask you a question. Why do we choose to stand on the mountaintop when the reality is, growth occurs during the storms of the valley?

Here's my perspective. People can see you easier on the mountain-top. So it fits the nomenclature of a narcissistic society that says, "I'm the focal point, I'm the spotlight. It's all about me."

Where are all the selfies taken anyway? On the mountaintop. "Here I am, man!" Nobody takes a picture in the valley. They don't want to remember the valley. There's not anything to share with people.

Just remember, your greatest growth is in the place you least want to be. I found hope where I least expected to discover it.

Again, circumstances don't leave you the way they found you.

Just ask yourself one simple question. Where have you grown the most as a person—the valley, or the mountaintop? You can't have growth without hope.

Take inventory of those perceived "hopeless" days. You'll be surprised what you may find.

Embracing a future and a hope takes work. You have to realize that maybe, just maybe, there's a potential to change the course of your life by allowing yourself to believe—believe your experiences have the capacity to shape you for the better.

When I look at the greatest times in my life, they've always come on the heels of despair. A bright future is predicated on the lessons we learn and the deliberate choices we make during times of struggle.

Your future isn't established on the mountaintop, on a clear day, as you write your grand plans in your leather-bound journal. (That's a great exercise though. Go for it.) Your future is established when you've run out of options.

That famous poet and former boxing champion, Mike Tyson, said it best: "Everybody has a plan until they get punched in the mouth."

But that's when you can make a choice.

So, my advice, if you're gonna dream, dream big! Former President Woodrow Wilson said, "We grow great by dreams."

Resist the temptation to cheapen your dreams with imitations of the real thing.

Ask a hundred people, "Have you ever imagined a better life?" I bet most would say yes! But I believe many equate their answer with, "Well, maybe I'll win the lottery, or maybe something good might happen."

Hope is not an emotion. Hope is not a feeling. Hope is not a wish.

Hope is a dynamic, transformative, life-changing quality. Hope is not temporal or transient. It is inside us. Always. Hope is not awarded based on who you are or what you do. Hope has no class status or social position. Some of the most hopeful people I have ever met are in jails. Conversely, I have met "free" people who have built self-constructed bars between them and life.

Please understand, hope is who we are. We were created with the capacity to hope. It is available to you right now.

It is ever-encompassing, affecting everything that you do, decide, feel, act on. It is ever-moving, ever-present, ever-involved in your life.

You know what I've noticed during twenty years as a college professor?

Many students looked for reasons to justify their incompetence. And you need to look no further than their parents. Most of us excuse our lack of growing. And so, instead of saying, "I'm going to make a choice to make hope active," we say, "Well, it's just the way it is. That's the way it was with my mother. That's the way it is on the job. I really can't change that."

What are you saying? How many times have you heard this, "There's nothing I can do." What we've done is taken even the potential for hope and said, "Hey, we have a cell made that's already down there waiting for you."

This explains the passage, "Hope deferred" makes the heart sick. When you relegate hope to the basement of human emotion, sick hearts only have the capacity to imagine the worst. Unhealthy minds become consumed with worry, doubt, anxiety, and fear.

Active hope

Do you feel hopeful?

Frankly, I don't care.

Why? Because hope is not merely an emotion that falls on you like glitter from a unicorn. And that's good news.

Hope is not passive; it's active. Traditionally, hope is defined as a feelings-based emotion. It goes like this … You buy the lottery ticket; you go to bed, you hope, you dream of riches, and imagine every problem solved. Then you wake up.

Since you didn't win, hope mysteriously vanishes. Poof! You throw away the ticket, and then the next time you have "hope" is when you buy the next lottery ticket.

And this view significantly minimizes the power of hope in our minds. It keeps us relegated to hope as just this kind of transient construct.

What I do care about is this: Are you beginning to intentionally place a demand on your heart and mind to believe for the best possible outcome?

What would happen if you elevated hope from the basement to the top floor? How might your thinking change if you began viewing hope as life changing?

Believing for better, the absolute best outcome, would begin to energize your spirit.

What are you waiting for?

Chapter 12

A PRESENT HOPE

This final chapter is intensely personal. My prayer is that these words spark hope, inspiring you to see what you do not. Today, I clearly see that hope was always there—right in the middle of the storm, right where I least expected it, right there at rock bottom.

I begin the final chapter of this book on an ominous anniversary, September 8, 2017. While that's just another day to most, it was on this exact day twenty-one years ago that Trina was pronounced dead. September 8th is always a rough one. I usually cry at some point, then text my older sons to celebrate the fact we made it another year. However, on this particular anniversary—I can't sleep.

I'm writing these words at 1:50 a.m. This was the exact time I was in the parking lot of the hospital with my friend Dwight. It was during this nightmare that Dwight first uttered those words of hope: "Rick, I don't know why Trina died, but I know God is sovereign."

There it is. The hope I longed for was right there, right there in that turbulent sea of emotions. Right there in the darkest hour of my life. Right there in the middle of hopelessness.

Hope is here

The purpose of this book is to help you discover *where* hope resides, and *how* to activate its dynamic and transformative force in your life.

We established in earlier chapters that hope resides within every human. Just because we don't "feel" hopeful, or have run out of reasons to hope, doesn't mean hope doesn't exist! Remember first and foremost: Hope resides in every one of us. Hope is a gift.

Discovering *how* to activate hope presents more of a daunting, though doable, challenge that will surprise you, as it has me. Now, keep in mind, I've had over two decades to think, reflect, and reenact every single scene from those unforgettable days of despair. I continue to arrive at the exact same conclusion:

At rock bottom … hope was staring me in the face the entire time.

Hope is always active within the human spirit. The problem arises when the brain becomes incapacitated by circumstances. In other words, the horrifically raw reality of September 8, 1996, overpowered my senses and neutralized my ability to consider other realities. Regardless, another reality existed.

Trina was gone. And, there was no human explanation that would satisfy me or bring her back. I couldn't fix this situation. I couldn't manipulate the variables. Sooner or later, if I were to survive physically, and maintain my sanity emotionally, I would have to trust. I had to trust in something bigger than myself.

I've believed in God for as long as I can remember, but completely trusting Him for stuff I can't fix or explain is an entirely different matter. Without fanfare, and perhaps unintentionally, Dwight had forced my hand. I had to decide. I couldn't escape. Right at ground zero there was hope in the simple words: "But I know God is sovereign."

The only thing that kept me somewhat sane was the reality that although something terrible happened, if I dared to trust, maybe … maybe I would see goodness again.

While it took me a long time to accept the "God is sovereign" part, I thought about Dwight's statement every single day for years. I began to note, as I gave myself permission to consider that God might be sovereign, two incongruent actions occurred in my heart: a fierce anger and an unshakable peace. I thought I was losing my mind.

Because I have a joyful disposition, I could fool most people, except those very close to me. I seethed in anger when I saw older couples enjoying life together. I felt rage when people said stupid things such as, "time heals all wounds" or "I know just how you feel. I lost my grandfather last year." Mostly, I was angry at God. My life was not fair, not right, not merciful, unwarranted, undeserved. My one-sided conversations filled that empty house many nights.

Oddly, after every venting session, a peace that to this day I can't explain would overwhelm me. I can still hear the voices vying for space in my shattered heart: "She's dead. But maybe. If God is sovereign. Maybe something good. Maybe there's something I can't see?"

Here was my hope:

I can't explain what happened.
But I'm going to make a choice.
I'm going to dare to continue living.
One breath and one step at a time.
Because maybe, just maybe, God does have a plan.
And that plan couldn't be any worse than what I'm experiencing now.

You see hope now, don't you!

Push yourself to hope

How many times have you heard someone say, "Maybe ... just maybe?"

Hope resides in the midst of the challenge. Hope resides at the breaking point. Hope resides when there is no meaning or explanation that can change the circumstances. Hope resides when you have no other choice, except the choice to say: "I wonder what might happen if...."

It doesn't have to take two decades to find hope. In fact, I've done my very best to help you understand and practice hope. Experiencing a time of crisis won't be easy. Helping a loved one see hope is not easy. It certainly won't be a time for champagne and strawberries. In fact, working through this process will punch you in the gut over and over again. But at some point, should you make a choice, your tears and screams will turn into maybes and dreams.

A note to agents of hope. Speak the truth in love. The worst thing you can do is coddle with empty and useless words. The blunt force of Dwight's words were so inescapable, I had no other choice but to face the facts.

Don't remove struggle from the hope equation. Without struggle you limit the desire to force the consideration for a change. Struggle is the only exercise that will force you to work through your emotions, to the realization that hope is more than an emotion.

We live in an outcome-oriented society, where everyone from the preacher to the president wants to fix it and fix it right now! And while that would be awesome, there are lessons that can only be taught in the valley.

Trust—for example—isn't formed in a casual relationship. And relationships worth anything must go through trials before trust can be earned. So then, why would we cheapen the process necessary for life-changing hope to be activated in our lives? Tension—circumstances, issues, conflict—are needed to force our hearts to consider offering our brain a different reality. Take away the valley and you take away the motivation for which to hope.

I clearly see that struggle incentivizes hope. Today, here's how I interpret Dwight's words when I am in a struggle:

I have no explanation for what's happening, but I must consider changing my present reality. I must dare to dream of a better outcome.

What is the best possible outcome?

Hope believes for the absolute best outcome. But what is "best"?

You've probably been thinking about the answer. *Do I place my hope on a specific outcome?*

Well, here's what we know: God is good and can work goodness in all circumstances.

Keep this in mind. How many times have you wished for something, got your wish, and regretted ever wishing in the first place? Demanding a specific outcome may not be in your best interest.

Had I demanded a specific outcome, I would still be in search of my purpose in life.

Remember when your parents said, "This is going to hurt you more than it hurts me"? Was that crazy, stupid logic, or what? As a parent today, I have a completely different answer. Those words are so true to me. As children, we sought escape from discipline. Our parents saw a much bigger picture than our "struggle." Our parents were intent on rearing great people who would do great things. As a child, hoping for a specific outcome, all I could see was a spanking, followed by kitchen duty all night. (Can't even eat my Swanson's Salisbury Steak TV dinner while watching *Lost in Space* and *Gilligan's Island!*)

The desired outcome may not have prepared me for adulthood. However, the best possible outcome, as difficult as it is to accept, will always be for your greater good. In the interim, the greater good does not appease your feelings or medicate your pain. That is why I challenge you to *believe* for the absolute best outcome.

What we're talking about here is control. Have you ever hoped for something, didn't get it, and to this day you're thankful it did not go your way? Do you ever thank God for *not* answering one of your prayers?

A large part of the struggle is a slowly developing shift from a convenient certainty to a what if? Simply stated, when we become fixated on a certain outcome, we limit our minds from considering other possibilities. All we desire is one specific outcome, which may or may not offer the results we're looking for.

On the other hand, when we hope for the best possible outcome, we're opening the door to dream in ways never imagined. The sky is the limit! Let me be graphically specific:

In 1996, my certain outcome was immediate relief of the pain for me and my boys. I cared about little else.

Little by little, daring to dream has produced a blessed family, a life, and an opportunity to help people around the world discover the hope within. I could have never experienced this by hoping for a "certain outcome."

I am not certain what the best possible outcome is. But I am certain that God has one in mind.

Hope defined

Throughout this book I have maintained one consistent definition of hope:

Hope is a quality of every human spirit that places
a transformative demand upon our heart to believe
for the absolute best outcome.

Rather than going through life with false hope, and setting ourselves up for disappointment, we can practice real, God-inspired hope.

True hope says, *No matter what happens, I'm going in search of possibilities and looking for the good in them. And not only that, I'm going to bring goodness into the lives of the people I encounter today!*

You have unlimited capacity for hope, because hope is a gift from God. But it's up to you to live a lifestyle of hope.

As hard as this might be for you to read, I want you to never forget: Your hope is right there in the valley. You control the level of hope in your life. If you'll dare to dream about a better, or even best outcome, the process of struggle will intensify. And while that may not be good news, the experience will help you clarify your next thought, your next word, and your next step.

This process is going to look different for each of us. Avoid the temptation of comparing your struggle to that of another.

As you close this book, remember one thing. The one who created you—God Almighty—has placed this dynamic gift called *hope* inside you. All you have to do is recognize it's there, and give yourself permission to dream of a better day.

Place a decisive demand upon yourself. Make today the day you cease being afraid to hope!

"For I know the plans I have for you," declares the Lord, *"plans to prosper you and not to harm you, plans to give you hope and a future"* (Jeremiah 29:11).

AUTHOR CONTACT

If you would like to contact Dr. Rick Rigsby, find out more information, purchase books, or request information about a speaking engagement, please contact:

Rick Rigsby Communications
972.649.4295
www.rickrigsby.com
connect@rickrigsby.com

Follow Rick!
www.facebook.com/DrRickRigsby
www.twitter.com/DrRickRigsby

ALSO AVAILABLE FROM RICK RIGSBY

Lessons from a Third Grade Dropout

USA Today, Amazon, and *The Wall Street Journal* best seller!

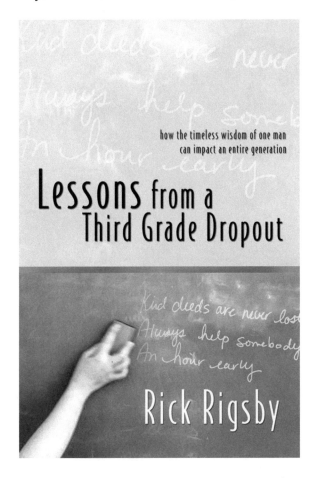

Go from making an impression to an impact with *Lessons from a Third Grade Dropout*. Six simple lessons modeled by an uneducated man were powerful enough to produce a Ph.D., a judge, and a lifetime of wisdom. Imagine how these lessons will impact you!

For more information or to purchase your copy of *Lessons from a Third Grade Dropout*, visit:

www.rickrigsby.com

RICKRIGSBY
COMMUNICATIONS

Over 130 million people worldwide watched *USA Today*, *The Wall Street Journal* and *Amazon* best-selling author Rick Rigsby speak about the transformative power of hope. The internationally recognized motivational speaker devotes his full attention to empowering people worldwide. Helping millions discover the true champions they were destined to become, Rick shares simple, yet profound principles of hope and perseverance learned from his father, a third-grade dropout.

The San Francisco Bay Area native is also a former award-winning journalist, who, following a successful television news career, earned a Master's degree from California State University, Chico, a Ph.D. from the University of Oregon, and in later years a Master's degree in Biblical Theology from Liberty University. During his years as a college professor at Texas A&M University, Dr. Rigsby also served as Life Skills Coordinator and chaplain for the Aggies football team.

In high demand among corporations, universities, schools, service organizations, and college and professional sports organizations, Dr. Rigsby offers common-sense wisdom to those desiring to rise to greater levels of excellence.